TOUCHSTONE

SECOND

STUDENT'S BOOK 4B

MICHAEL MCCARTHY

JEANNE MCCARTEN

HELEN SANDIFORD

CAMBRIDGE
UNIVERSITY PRESS

CAMBRIDGE
UNIVERSITY PRESS

32 Avenue of the Americas, New York, NY 10013-2473, USA

Cambridge University Press is part of the University of Cambridge.

It furthers the University's mission by disseminating knowledge in the pursuit of education, learning and research at the highest international levels of excellence.

www.cambridge.org
Information on this title: www.cambridge.org/9781107667631

© Cambridge University Press 2005, 2014

First published 2005
Second Edition 2014

Printed in Hong Kong, China, by Golden Cup Printing Company Limited

A catalog record for this publication is available from the British Library.

ISBN 978-1-107-68043-2 Student's Book
ISBN 978-1-107-62430-6 Student's Book A
ISBN 978-1-107-63748-1 Student's Book B
ISBN 978-1-107-68275-7 Workbook
ISBN 978-1-107-62708-6 Workbook A
ISBN 978-1-107-69602-0 Workbook B
ISBN 978-1-107-66152-3 Full Contact
ISBN 978-1-107-67936-8 Full Contact A
ISBN 978-1-107-66763-1 Full Contact B
ISBN 978-1-107-68151-4 Teacher's Edition with Assessment Audio CD/CD-ROM
ISBN 978-1-107-61272-3 Class Audio CDs (4)

Additional resources for this publication at www.cambridge.org/touchstone2

Touchstone Second Edition has benefited from extensive development research. The authors and publishers would like to extend their thanks to the following reviewers and consultants for their valuable insights and suggestions:

Ana Lúcia da Costa Maia de Almeida and Mônica da Costa Monteiro de Souza from **IBEU**, Rio de Janeiro, Brazil; Andreza Cristiane Melo do Lago from **Magic English School,** Manaus, Brazil; Magaly Mendes Lemos from **ICBEU**, São José dos Campos, Brazil; Maria Lucia Zaorob, São Paulo, Brazil; Patricia McKay Aronis from **CEL LEP**, São Paulo, Brazil; Carlos Gontow, São Paulo, Brazil; Christiane Augusto Gomes da Silva from **Colégio Visconde de Porto Seguro,** São Paulo, Brazil; Silvana Fontana from **Lord's Idiomas**, São Paulo, Brazil; Alexander Fabiano Morishigue from **Speed Up Idiomas**, Jales, Brazil; Elisabeth Blom from **Casa Thomas Jefferson**, Brasília, Brazil; Michelle Dear from **International Academy of English**, Toronto, ON, Canada; Walter Duarte Marin, Laura Hurtado Portela, Jorge Quiroga, and Ricardo Suarez, from **Centro Colombo Americano**, Bogotá, Colombia; Jhon Jairo Castaneda Macias from **Praxis English Academy**, Bucaramanga, Colombia; Gloria Liliana Moreno Vizcaino from **Universidad Santo Tomas**, Bogotá, Colombia; Elizabeth Ortiz from **Copol English Institute (COPEI)**, Guayaquil, Ecuador; Henry Foster from **Kyoto Tachibana University**, Kyoto, Japan; Steven Kirk from **Tokyo University**, Tokyo, Japan; J. Lake from **Fukuoka Woman's University**, Fukuoka, Japan; Etsuko Yoshida from **Mie University**, Mie, Japan; B. Bricklin Zeff from **Hokkai Gakuen University**, Hokkaido, Japan; Ziad Abu-Hamatteh from **Al-Balqa' Applied University**, Al-Salt, Jordan; Roxana Pérez Flores from **Universidad Autonoma de Coahuila Language Center**, Saltillo, Mexico; Kim Alejandro Soriano Jimenez from **Universidad Politecnica de Altamira**, Altamira, Mexico; Tere Calderon Rosas from **Universidad Autonoma Metropolitana Campus Iztapalapa**, Mexico City, Mexico; Lilia Bondareva, Polina Ermakova, and Elena Frumina, from **National Research Technical University MISiS**, Moscow, Russia; Dianne C. Ellis from **Kyung Hee University**, Gyeonggi-do, South Korea; Jason M. Ham and Victoria Jo from **Institute of Foreign Language Education, Catholic University of Korea**, Gyeonggi-do, South Korea; Shaun Manning from **Hankuk University of Foreign Studies**, Seoul, South Korea; Natalie Renton from **Busan National University of Education**, Busan, South Korea; Chris Soutter from **Busan University of Foreign Studies**, Busan, South Korea; Andrew Cook from **Dong A University**, Busan, South Korea; Raymond Wowk from **Daejin University**, Gyeonggi-do, South Korea; Ming-Hui Hsieh and Jessie Huang from **National Central University**, Zhongli, Taiwan; Kim Phillips from **Chinese Culture University**, Taipei, Taiwan; Alex Shih from **China University of Technology**, Taipei Ta-Liao Township, Taiwan; Porntip Bodeepongse from **Thaksin University**, Songkhla, Thailand; Nattaya Puakpong and Pannathon Sangarun from **Suranaree University of Technology**, Nakhon Ratchasima, Thailand; Barbara Richards, Gloria Stewner-Manzanares, and Caroline Thompson, from **Montgomery College**, Rockville, MD, USA; Kerry Vrabel from **Gateway Community College**, Phoenix, AZ, USA.

Touchstone Second Edition authors and publishers would also like to thank the following individuals and institutions who have provided excellent feedback and support on *Touchstone Blended*:

Gordon Lewis, Vice President, Laureate Languages and Chris Johnson, Director, Laureate English Programs, Latin America from **Laureate International Universities**; **Universidad de las Americas**, Santiago, Chile; **University of Victoria**, Paris, France; **Universidad Technólogica Centroamericana**, Honduras; **Institut Universitaire de Casablanca**, Morocco; **Universidad Peruana de Ciencias Aplicadas**, Lima, Peru; **CIBERTEC**, Peru; **National Research Technical University (MiSIS)**, Moscow, Russia; **Institut Obert de Catalunya (IOC)**, Barcelona, Spain; Sedat Çilingir, Burcu Tezcan Ünal, and Didem Mutçalıoğlu from **İstanbul Bilgi Üniversitesi**, Istanbul, Turkey.

Touchstone Second Edition authors and publishers would also like to thank the following contributors to *Touchstone Second Edition*:

Sue Aldcorn, Frances Amrani, Deborah Gordon, Lisa Hutchins, Nancy Jordan, Steven Kirk, Genevieve Kocienda, Geraldine Mark, Julianna Nielsen, Kathryn O'Dell, Ellen Shaw, Kristin Sherman, Luis Silva Susa, Mary Vaughn, Kerry S. Vrabel, and Eric Zuarino.

Authors' Acknowledgments

The authors would like to thank all the Cambridge University Press staff and freelancers who were involved in the creation of *Touchstone Second Edition*. In addition, they would like to acknowledge a huge debt of gratitude that they owe to two people: Mary Vaughn, for her role in creating *Touchstone First Edition* and for being a constant source of wisdom ever since, and Bryan Fletcher, who also had the vision that has led to the success of *Touchstone Blended Learning*.

Helen Sandiford would like to thank her family for their love and support, especially her husband Bryan.

The author team would also like to thank each other, for the joy of working together, sharing the same professional dedication, and for the mutual support and friendship.

Finally, the authors would like to thank our dear friend Alejandro Martinez, Global Training Manager, who sadly passed away in 2012. He is greatly missed by all who had the pleasure to work with him. Alex was a huge supporter of *Touchstone* and everyone is deeply grateful to him for his contribution to its success.

Touchstone Level 4B Contents and learning outcomes

Interaction	Skills				Self study
Conversation strategies	**Listening**	**Reading**	**Writing**	**Free talk**	**Vocabulary notebook**
• Speak informally in "shorter sentences" • Use expressions like *Uh-oh!* and *Oops!* when something goes wrong	***Wedding on a budget*** • Listen to people plan a wedding; check what they agree on and what they'll do themselves ***Fix it!*** • Match conversations with pictures; then check which problems were solved	***Developing your problem-solving skills*** • An article about an interesting problem-solving technique	***A good solution*** • Write a proposal presenting a solution to a problem at work • Format for presenting a problem and its solution	***Who gets help with something?*** • Class activity: Ask and answer questions to find out who gets help	***Damaged goods*** • Find out if new words have different forms that can express the same idea, and use them in sentences
• Use expressions such as *That reminds me (of) . . .* to share experiences • Use *like* informally in conversation	***Similar experiences*** • Listen to two people share experiences, and number the incidents in order; then answer questions ***Good and bad apologies*** • Listen to conversations; match the people to the apologies; then decide if they were effective	***Apologies: The key to maintaining friendship*** • An article about the importance of apologizing and suggesting ways to do so	***A note of apology*** • Write an email apologizing for something • Expressions for writing a note of apology	***How did you react?*** • Group work: Tell a story about an incident, and listen and respond to classmates' stories	***People watching*** • Learn new vocabulary by making a connection with something or someone you know, and write true sentences
• Report the content of conversations you have had • Quote other people or other sources of information	***Who's materialistic?*** • Listen to someone answer questions, and take notes; then report his answers ***I couldn't live without . . .*** • Listen to four people talk about things they couldn't live without, and complete a chart; then listen and write responses to opinions	***This Stuff's Gotta Go!*** • A blog post about a woman who declutters her home	***I couldn't live without . . .*** • Write an article about your classmates and things they feel they couldn't live without • Use of reporting verbs for direct speech and reported speech	***Material things*** • Pair work: Ask and answer questions about material things	***Get rich!*** • When you learn a new word, notice its collocations – the words that are used with it

Checkpoint Units 7–9   pages 95–96

• Use tag questions to soften advice and give encouragement • Answer difficult questions with expressions like *It's hard to say*	***Great advice*** • Listen to a conversation and answer questions ***Success is . . .*** • Listen to four conversations about success, and complete a chart	***Three Child Stars Who Beat the Odds*** • A magazine article about actors who have managed to avoid "Child Star Syndrome"	***A success story*** • Write a paragraph about someone you know who has achieved success, and explain why that person became successful • Topic and supporting sentences in a paragraph	***Quotations*** • Group work: Define success	***Do your best!*** • Learn new idioms by writing example sentences that explain or clarify meaning
• Refer back to points made earlier in a conversation • Use more formal vague expressions like *and so forth* and *etc.*	***Trends in the workplace*** • Listen to conversations about trends, and identify advantages and disadvantages ***Trends in technology*** • Listen to four people talk about trends, and write notes on their views	***The Internet – The new pathway to success?*** • An article about the recent trend of using the Internet to become successful	***Trends in technology*** • Write a comment on a web article about trends in technology • Expressions for describing trends	***What's trending?*** • Group work: Discuss trends	***Try to explain it!*** • Write definitions in your own words to help you learn the meaning of new words and expressions
• Introduce what you say with expressions like *The best part was (that) . . .* • Use *I don't know if . . .* to introduce a statement and involve the other person in the topic	***An interesting job*** • Listen to a personal trainer talk about her job; write notes ***A fabulous opportunity!*** • Complete a job ad, and listen to check and answer questions	***Ace that Interview!*** • An article about how to answer the most common questions in job interviews	***A fabulous opportunity!*** • Write a cover letter in response to an ad • Format for writing a cover letter for a job application	***The best person for the job*** • Group work: Interview the members of your group for a job	***From accountant to zoologist*** • When you learn a new word, learn other words with the same root as well as common collocations to expand your vocabulary quickly

Checkpoint Units 10–12   pages 127–128

v

Useful language for . . .

Working in groups

We're ready now, aren't we?

Are we ready? Let's get started.

Haven't I interviewed you already?

I've already interviewed you, haven't I?

Where are we?

We're on number _____ .

We haven't quite finished yet.

Neither have we.

We still need more time – just a few more minutes.

So do we.

One interesting thing we found out was that _____ .

_____ told us that _____ .

Checking with the teacher

Would it be all right if I missed our class tomorrow? I have to _____ .

I'm sorry I missed the last class. What do I need to do to catch up?

When are we supposed to hand in our homework?

Excuse me. My homework needs to be checked.

I'm sorry. I haven't finished my homework. I was going to do it last night, but _____ .

Will we be reviewing this before the next test?

"_____" means "_____," doesn't it? It's a regular verb, isn't it?

I'm not sure I understand what we're supposed to do. Could you explain the activity again, please?

Could I please be excused? I'll be right back.

Problem solving

 Can Do! In this unit, you learn how to . . .

Lesson A
- Talk about things others do for you using *get* and *have*

Lesson B
- Describe household problems using *need* + passive infinitive or *need* + verb + *-ing*

Lesson C
- Speak informally in "shorter sentences"
- Use expressions like *Uh-oh* and *Ouch* when things go wrong

Lesson D
- Read an article about problem solving
- Write a proposal on how to solve a problem

1. a camera store

2. an optometrist

3. a copy shop

4. a dry cleaner's

5. a garage

6. a hair salon

Before you begin . . .

Where do you go when . . .

- you need a haircut?
- you need new glasses?
- you need some photocopies?

- there's a big stain on your jacket?
- you need a memory card for your camera?
- your car or motorcycle breaks down?

Do it yourself!

We asked people what jobs they do themselves in order to save money. Here's what they said:

Have you ever cut your own hair to save money?

"I have, actually. But it looked so bad that I went to the most expensive place in town and had a hairdresser cut it again. I'll never try that again! Now I always get it cut professionally at a good hair salon, though I get a friend to cut my bangs occasionally. That saves me some money."
—Min-sook Kim, Seoul, South Korea

Do you do your own car repairs?

"Well, I can do routine things like put oil in the car. But, to be honest, I get my brother to fix most things. And if there's something seriously wrong with my car, I have my uncle take a look at it at his garage. I can get it fixed there pretty cheaply. I also have it serviced there once a year."
—Marcus Aldóvar, Bogotá, Colombia

Do you do your own home decorating?

"My wife and I are having a new house built right now, but we're going to do all the painting and decorating ourselves. We've done it before. My sister's an interior designer, so we'll have her choose the colors and get her to pick out curtains, too. She's got great taste."
—Martin and Jill Snow Calgary, Canada

Do you ever do your own repairs around the house?

"Not anymore! Once I tried fixing the dishwasher myself because I didn't want to pay to have someone come and repair it. But I didn't realize I had to turn off the water first. So I fixed the problem, but I flooded the entire apartment! And it cost a fortune to have the water damage repaired."
—Bella Clark, Miami, U.S.A.

1 Getting started

A Which of these things do you do yourself? What other jobs do you do? Make a class list.

cut your own hair	do your own repairs around the house	put oil in your car
decorate your home	fix your computer	

B 🔊 3.01 Listen. What jobs have the people above done themselves? Were they successful?

 C Complete *b* so it has a similar meaning to *a*. Use the interviews to help you.

1. a. I ask my brother to fix things.
   b. I _____ my brother _____ things.

2. a. We'll ask my sister to choose the colors.
   b. We'll _____ my sister _____ the colors.

3. a. Someone in a salon cuts my hair.
   b. I _____ my hair _____ at a good salon.

4. a. I had to pay someone to repair the damage.
   b. I had to _____ the damage _____ .

2 Grammar Causative *get* and *have* ◀)) 3.02

Extra practice p. 146

You can use *get* and *have* to talk about asking other people to do things for you.

When you want to show who you ask, you can use *get* + *someone* + *to* + verb or *have* + *someone* + verb.

I **get my brother to fix** my car.
We'll **get my sister to choose** colors for our house.
My hair looked bad, so I **had a hairdresser cut** it again.
I didn't pay to **have someone repair** my dishwasher.

When who you ask is not important, use *get* or *have* + *something* + past participle.

I **get my car fixed** at my uncle's garage.
I always **get my hair cut** professionally.
We're **having a new house built** now.
It cost a lot to **have the water damage repaired**.

About you **A** Circle the correct options, and write your own answers to the questions. Then ask and answer the questions with a partner.

1. Do you usually get your hair **cut** / **to cut** professionally? How often do you get it cut?
   I always get my hair cut professionally. I usually . . .
2. Have you ever **had** / **got** a friend cut your hair? How did it turn out?
3. Do you have a bicycle, motorcycle, or car? Where do you get it **fixed** / **fix**?
4. If you had a flat tire, would you get someone **to change** / **change** it for you or do it yourself?
5. Do you ever take clothes to the dry cleaner's? Is it expensive to get things **to clean** / **cleaned**?
6. Do you iron your own clothes? Do you ever get someone **iron** / **to iron** things for you?
7. Do you ever fix things around the house, or do you have small jobs **done** / **do** by a professional?

B **Pair work** What things do people often have done professionally? Make a list. Then discuss each item on your list. Where do you get them done? Is it expensive?

"Well, people often get their cars cleaned professionally. We get a local company to clean ours."

3 Listening Wedding on a budget

A ◀)) 3.03 Listen to Molly and Mark talk about things they need to do to get ready for their wedding. What topics do they agree on? Check (✓) the boxes.

1 ☐

2 ☐

3 ☐

4 ☐

5 ☐

6 ☐

B ◀)) 3.03 Listen again. Which things are Molly and Mark going to have done professionally? Which things are they or their families going to do themselves? Make two lists.

About you **C** **Pair work** Imagine you are organizing a wedding or a family event. What things would you do? What would you have someone else do?

"If I had to organize a wedding, I'd get my friends to take the photos."

1 Building language

A 🔊 3.04 Listen. What is Isaac good at fixing? Practice the conversation.

Anna Isaac, something's wrong with the shower. It won't turn off completely. It keeps dripping.

Isaac Yeah? Maybe the showerhead needs replacing.

Anna Oh, it's probably just a washer or something that needs to be replaced. Can you take a look at it?

Isaac Me? I'm not a plumber. I don't even know what's wrong with it.

Anna I know. But you're always so good when the TV needs to be fixed. You know, when the screen needs adjusting.

Isaac Yeah, well, that's an emergency!

Figure it out B Find two different ways to say *We need to replace the showerhead* in the conversation. Complete the sentences below.

The showerhead needs _____ .   **OR**   The showerhead needs _____ .

2 Grammar *need* + passive infinitive and *need* + verb + *-ing* 🔊 3.05

Extra practice p. 146

You can use *need* to talk about things that should be done.

need + passive infinitive	*need* + verb + *-ing*
The TV needs **to be fixed**.	The TV needs **fixing**.
The screen needs **to be adjusted**.	The screen needs **adjusting**.

The structure *need* + verb + *-ing* is mainly used for everyday chores like fixing, changing, cleaning, adjusting, replacing, recharging, etc.

✗ Common errors

Don't use *I need* + verb + *-ing* to say what you are going to do.

*I **need to change** my tire.* (NOT *I need changing my tire.*)

A Complete the sentences below in two ways. Use *need* + passive infinitive and *need* + verb + *-ing*. Compare with a partner.

1. My computer's very slow. Maybe the memory *needs to be upgraded / needs upgrading* (upgrade).
2. There's a problem with our car. The brakes _____ (adjust).
3. I can't make any calls right now because my cell phone _____ (recharge).
4. My camera is always going dead. The batteries _____ (replace) constantly.
5. The closet light won't turn on. The bulb _____ (change or tighten).
6. Our air conditioner isn't working very well. Maybe the filter _____ (clean).
7. One of our bookshelves is falling apart. It _____ (fix).
8. There are bills and papers all over the house. They _____ (file).
9. Our piano is out of tune. It really _____ (tune).

About you B **Pair work** Are any of the sentences above true for you? Do you have any similar problems?

A I don't have any problems with my computer, but some software needs to be upgraded.

B Yeah? My keyboard needs replacing. Some of the keys aren't working properly.

③ Building vocabulary

A Anna is pointing out more problems to Isaac. Can you guess the things she's talking about? Complete the sentences below. Then compare answers with a partner.

1. "The ___microwave___ **isn't working**. Nothing's happening. It **won't turn on**."
2. "The _____ **is leaking**. And there's **a dent** in the door."
3. "The _____ **keeps flickering** on and off. And I **got a shock** from it."
4. "The _____ is **loose**. If it **falls off**, we won't be able to open the door."
5. "The ceiling _____ **is making a funny noise**."
6. "The _____ has **a** big **scratch** on it."
7. "That _____ is **torn**. And look – there's **a** big **hole** in the other one."
8. "There's **a** coffee **stain** on the _____ ."
9. "The _____ is a half hour **slow**. Actually, it **stopped**. The battery must be **dead**."

Word sort **B** Can you think of two items for each of the problems below? Do you have any things like these that need to be fixed? Tell a partner.

Things that often . . .	Things that are often . . .	Things that often have . . .
leak: *refrigerator, pen*	scratched:	a dent in them:
fall off:	torn:	a stain on them:
make a funny noise:	loose:	a hole in them:
won't turn on:	slow:	dead batteries:

Vocabulary notebook p. 74

C Pair work Make a "to do" list for Anna and Isaac, and prioritize each task. How can they get the problems fixed? Which things need to be done right away?

A They need to get their microwave fixed. They should get someone to look at it.

B Actually, I think it probably needs to be replaced.

1 Conversation strategy   Speaking in "shorter sentences"

A What kinds of jobs do you get your friends to help you with? Make a class list.

B 🔊 3.06 Listen. What are Kayla and Hector trying to do? Do they succeed?

Kayla	Hi, there. . . . Ooh! Want some help?
Hector	Sure. Just take that end. Got it?
Kayla	Yeah. Think so. Oops! Wait a second.
Hector	OK. . . . Ready? One, two, three, lift.
Kayla	Ooh, it's heavy! . . . Ow! Just broke a nail.
Hector	Ouch! You OK?
Kayla	Yeah. But hurry up!
Hector	There. Shoot! It's not straight.
Kayla	Want me to fix it? . . . Better?
Hector	Yeah, . . . up a bit on the left.
Kayla	There you go. Done.
Hector	Thanks. Like it?
Kayla	Love it. It looks good. Really good.
Hector	Want some coffee?
Kayla	No, thanks. Can't drink it. Got any soda?
Hector	Sure. . . . Uh-oh! Don't have any. Sorry.

C Notice how Kayla and Hector speak in "shorter sentences." They leave out words like *I* or *you* and verbs like *do*, *be*, and *have*. People often do this in informal conversations, especially when it's clear who or what they're talking about. Find more examples.

"(Do you) Want some help?"
"(I) Just broke a nail."
"(Are) You OK?"

D Rewrite the conversation with shorter sentences. Compare with a partner and practice.

A   Do you need this screwdriver? Here it is.
B   Thanks. I can't get this shelf off the wall.
A   Do you want me to try getting it off for you?
B   Yes, thanks. Are you sure you've got time?
A   Yes. . . . OK. That's done. Do you need help with anything else?
B   Thank you. No, there's nothing else. Would you like a drink?
A   I'd love one. Have you got any green tea?

2 Strategy plus *Uh-oh!*

Ow!

You can use words like *Uh-oh!* and *Oops!* when something goes wrong.

Ooh!	=	when you see a problem
Uh-oh!	=	when you suddenly discover a problem
Oops! / Whoops!	=	when you make a small mistake
Ow! / Ouch!	=	"That hurt." / "It sounds like that hurt."
Shoot!	=	"Oh, no!" (a general reaction)
Ugh! / Yuck!	=	"It's disgusting."

In conversation

Ooh!
Uh-oh!
Ow!
Oops! / Whoops!
Ugh! / Yuck!
Shoot!
Ouch!

Write an expression you can use in each situation. Can you think of more expressions you can use? Compare with a partner.

1. You drop a hammer on your toe. ___Ow!___
2. You miss an important phone call. _____
3. You spill coffee on the table. _____
4. A friend tells you how she broke her arm. _____
5. You realized you just missed a class. _____
6. You put too much sugar in your coffee. _____

3 Speaking naturally Short question and statement intonation

Questions: *Ready?* *OK?*   **Statements:** *Ready.* *OK.*

A ◀)) 3.07 **Listen and repeat the words above. Notice the rising intonation for short questions and falling intonation for short statements.**

B ◀)) 3.08 **Listen. Is each sentence a question or a statement? Add a question mark (?) or a period (.).**

1. Better __?__
2. Got it ____
3. Broke a nail ____
4. Left a bit ____
5. Done ____
6. You need help ____
7. Got a drink ____
8. Ready ____

4 Listening and strategies Fix it!

A ◀)) 3.09 **Listen to four people talk about things they are trying to fix. Number the pictures 1 to 4. There is one extra picture.**

☐ _____ ☐ _____ ☐ _____ ☐ _____ ☐ _____

B ◀)) 3.09 **Listen again. Do they solve the problems? Write *Yes* or *No* on the lines.**

C Pair work Choose one of the pictures, and write a conversation using shorter sentences. Perform it to another pair. Can they guess what activity you are doing?

A You OK? Need some help?
B Yeah. This just fell off. Can't get it back on.

(((• **Sounds right** p. 138

71

1 Reading

A What's the best way to solve problems? Do you do any of these things? Tell the class.

☐ Ignore the problem and do something else.
☐ Brainstorm or make a mind map.
☐ Watch your favorite comedy before you start.

☐ Try different solutions until one works.
☐ Concentrate on the problem in a quiet place.
☐ Take enough time to think of ideas.

B Read the article. Which of the ideas above are recommended?

> **Reading tip**
>
> As you read, highlight two or three useful collocations you can use in your daily life, such as *tackle an assignment*, *solve a problem*.

DEVELOPING YOUR PROBLEM-SOLVING SKILLS

Can you solve these two classic puzzles?

1. **You have a candle and a box of thumbtacks. How can you attach the candle to the wall?**
2. **Two ropes hang from the ceiling. They're too far apart for you to hold both ropes at the same time. They need to be tied together. How can you tie them?**

Daily life presents us with a huge variety of problems, many of which seem to have no ready or easy solutions. From deciding which apartment to rent to figuring out how to tackle an assignment at school or work, or even handling relationships, day in and day out we have to find ways of solving our problems. Techniques like brainstorming, mind mapping, or listing the pros and cons of different options take an analytical approach and involve "left-brain" thinking. While these techniques can be successful and lead to solutions, good problem solvers tend to switch between this analytical (left-brain) thinking and a more creative and emotional (right-brain) approach.

However, recent research into the brain's behavior while problem solving suggests that traditional techniques for solving problems — concentrating on a task and focusing on finding a solution — may not be the most effective after all. What might be more significant is simply inspiration — that sudden "aha" moment when the solution to a problem appears.

Neuroscientist Mark Beeman's studies into brain activity show that inspiration happens in the brain's right temporal lobe — an area that *isn't* associated with concentration at all. It's an area of the brain that's responsible for facial recognition, connecting memories, and understanding language. Brain imaging scans show a constant low frequency activity in this area, indicating that it's always quietly working in the background of our minds. Beeman suggests that when you're *not* focused on a particular task, for example when you're relaxing before bed or taking a walk, the constant brain "chatter" quiets and the temporal lobe can make connections between distant, unrelated memories. Less than two seconds before inspiration hits, there's a burst of high frequency activity, and eureka! You have a solution.

Now that scientists know *where* problem solving happens, they're beginning to understand *how* to improve it. In tests, people solved more puzzles after watching funny videos than after watching boring or scary movies. This is probably because the people who were watching the funny videos were more relaxed, thus allowing the temporal lobe to perform more effectively.

People were also more likely to solve the puzzles in an "aha!" moment than by analysis. Beeman suggests this is because when people are happy, their brains notice a wider range of information.

The conclusion seems to be that if you want to solve a problem, don't focus on it. Let your brain be quiet and the answer might arrive in a sudden flash of inspiration. Now try solving the problems in the box again. Aha – did it work?

ANSWERS:
1. Tack the box to the wall and stand the candle on top.
2. Attach something heavy to one of the ropes and swing it toward the other.

C Are the statements below true or false according to the article? Check (✓) the boxes.

	True	False
1. Good problem solvers use the right side of their brain more than the left.	☐	☐
2. The right temporal lobe is active all the time.	☐	☐
3. When the brain is busy, it makes faster connections between memories.	☐	☐
4. Watching videos makes it more difficult for people to solve problems.	☐	☐
5. When people are in a good mood, they are more able to solve problems.	☐	☐

D Read the article again. Answer the questions. Then discuss with a partner.

1. What does the latest research say about the traditional techniques for problem solving?
2. What are three things that happen in the brain's right temporal lobe?
3. How does brain activity change in the moments before you find a solution to a problem?
4. What kind of videos should you watch to improve your problem-solving ability?
5. What *shouldn't* you do if you want to make inspiration more likely to arrive?

2 Speaking and writing A good solution

A Group work Read the problem below. Discuss your ideas and agree on a solution.

The events management company that you work for is holding a Movie Awards Ceremony in your city five days from now. Famous actors and directors are attending as well as the international media. However, you have just received very bad news. A serious fire has completely destroyed the concert hall where the event is supposed to be. The Awards Committee wants to cancel the event, but you will lose millions of dollars, and the city is depending on the awards to boost its tourism industry. What can you do to save your event?

B Read the proposal below. Then write your own proposal persuading the Awards Committee to agree to your ideas. Describe the problem and how you plan to solve it.

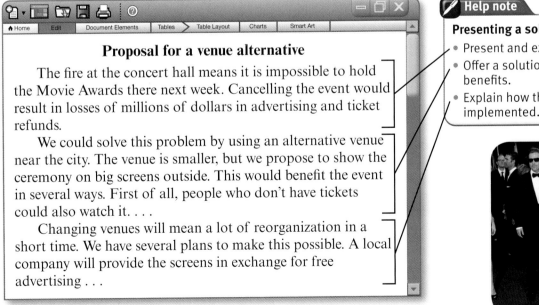

Proposal for a venue alternative

The fire at the concert hall means it is impossible to hold the Movie Awards there next week. Cancelling the event would result in losses of millions of dollars in advertising and ticket refunds.

We could solve this problem by using an alternative venue near the city. The venue is smaller, but we propose to show the ceremony on big screens outside. This would benefit the event in several ways. First of all, people who don't have tickets could also watch it. . . .

Changing venues will mean a lot of reorganization in a short time. We have several plans to make this possible. A local company will provide the screens in exchange for free advertising . . .

Help note

Presenting a solution
- Present and explain the problem.
- Offer a solution and explain its benefits.
- Explain how the solution will be implemented.

C Read your classmates' proposals. What are the best ideas?

Free talk p. 132

Learning tip *Different forms of the same word*

When you learn a new word, find out what type of word it is – a verb, a noun, an adjective, etc. – and whether it has a different form that can express the same idea.

There's a <u>leak</u> in the bathroom. *(noun)*	There's a <u>scratch</u> on this DVD. *(noun)*
The pipe is <u>leaking</u>. *(verb)*	This DVD is <u>scratched</u>. *(adjective)*

1 What's wrong with Mark's things? Complete the two sentences for each problem. Use the words in the box.

> dent / dented   leak / leaking   scratch / scratched   stain / stained   tear / torn

1. There's a big _____ in the wheel of Mark's mountain bike. It's _____ .
2. There's a dark _____ on his T-shirt. It's _____ .
3. His shorts are _____ . There's a _____ in them.
4. His sunglasses are _____ . They have a _____ on them.
5. There's a _____ in his water bottle. It's _____ .

2 **Word builder** Find out the meaning of the underlined words below. Then rewrite the sentences using a different form of the underlined word.

1. My coffee mug is <u>chipped</u>.
2. The mirror is <u>cracked</u>.
3. There's a lot of <u>rust</u> on my car.
4. There's a lot of <u>mold</u> in my shower.

 On your own

Look around your home. What problems are there? Label each one. Remove the label when the problem is fixed!

✓ Can Do! Now I can . . .

☑ I can . . .   ？ I need to review how to . . .

- ☐ talk about things you have other people do for you.
- ☐ talk about things that need to be fixed.
- ☐ use short sentences in informal conversations.
- ☐ use expressions like *Uh-oh* when something goes wrong.

- ☐ understand a conversation about planning an event.
- ☐ understand people talking about things they need to fix.
- ☐ read an article about problem-solving skills.
- ☐ write a proposal presenting a solution to a problem.

Behavior

✓ **Can Do!** In this unit, you learn how to . . .

Lesson A
- Talk hypothetically about the past using *would have*, *should have*, and *could have*

Lesson B
- Describe emotions and personal qualities
- Speculate about the past using *must have*, *may have*, *might have*, and *could have*

Lesson C
- Share experiences using expressions like *That reminds me (of)*
- Use *like* in conversation

Lesson D
- Read an article on making apologies
- Write a note of apology

1

2

3

4

Before you begin . . .

Can you think of any situations that would make you . . .

- hug someone?
- laugh out loud?
- sulk? mope?
- lose your temper?
- hang up on someone?
- get mad and yell at someone?

Last night this guy called, trying to sell me something. Normally, I would have been more polite – you know, I would have just said no and then hung up. But he was the fourth caller in three hours, and it was after 10:00. So I just lost it. I yelled at him for several minutes, and I finally hung up on him. At that point, I couldn't have done much else, I don't think, because I was too mad. I know I shouldn't have lost my temper – he was just doing his job – but, I mean, what would you have done? Would you have gotten mad? I suppose I could have apologized. Or I could have asked him to put me on their "do not call" list. Actually, that's what I should have done. I'll do that next time!

1 Getting started

A What kinds of unwanted calls do people get? If you get unwanted calls, what do you say?

"Well, I get calls from people who are trying to sell things. I usually say . . . "

B ◀)) 3.10 Listen to Amelia tell her friends about a phone call she got last night. What made Amelia lose her temper? How did she behave toward the caller?

Figure
it out **C** What does Amelia say about her behavior? What do you think? Complete the sentences. Then compare with a partner.

Amelia says . . .
1. I shouldn't _____ .
2. I could _____ .
3. What would you _____ ?

I think . . .
4. Amelia shouldn't _____ .
5. I would _____ .
6. I wouldn't _____ .

2 Speaking naturally   Reduction of *have* in past modals

Amelia should **have** been more polite. (should'**ve**)	She couldn't **have** done much else. (couldn't'**ve**)
She shouldn't **have** lost her temper. (shouldn't'**ve**)	I would **have** said no and hung up. (would'**ve**)
She could **have** apologized. (could'**ve**)	I wouldn't **have** yelled at him. (wouldn't'**ve**)

A ◀)) 3.11 Listen and repeat the sentences. Notice the reduction of *have*.

About
you **B** **Pair work** Which sentences do you agree with? Tell a partner.

A *Amelia really should have been more polite.*
B *I agree. She shouldn't have lost her temper.*

3 **Grammar** Past modals ◄)) 3.12

Extra practice p. 147

You can use *would* / *should* / *could* + *have* + past participle to talk hypothetically about the past.

Imagine your behavior in a situation:	What **would** you **have done**? I **would have said** no politely. I **wouldn't have lost** my temper.	**Would** you **have gotten** mad? Yes, I probably **would have**.	
Say what was the right thing to do:	What **should** she **have done**? She **should have said** no politely. She **shouldn't have yelled** at him.	**Should** she **have yelled** at him? No, she really **shouldn't have**.	
Say what other possibilities there were:	What else **could** she **have done**? She **could have told** him not to call again. She **couldn't have done** much else.	**Could** she **have been** more polite? I feel she **could have**.	

In conversation

I would is 20 times more common than *I'd* with past modals.

About you **A** Read the situations and complete the questions. Then write your own answers. How many ideas can you think of?

1. Josh saw someone in a parked car throw litter out of the window. He picked it up and threw it right back into the car. Should he ___have thrown___ (throw) it back in? What else could he _____ (do)?
He shouldn't have thrown it back in the car. He could have . . .

2. Sofia was late for a meeting because she slept late. She called the office and told them she'd gotten tied up in traffic. What other excuses could she _____ (make)? Should she _____ (tell) the truth?

3. Dan was in a parking lot. He saw a driver accidentally hit another car. The driver left thinking that no one had seen him. What could Dan _____ (say)? What should the driver _____ (do)?

4. Katy saw her boyfriend talking to another girl. She called him, told him she didn't want to see him again, and then hung up. Should she _____ (hang) up? How else could she _____ (react)?

5. Andrea's friends were making too much noise late one night. Her father yelled at them and asked them to leave. Should he _____ (lose) his temper? How else could he _____ (respond)?

6. Jun was in a café. A girl pushed past him and spilled his coffee on him. She just walked away. Could she _____ (offer) to clean it up? Should she _____ (apologize)?

B **Pair work** Compare your ideas and discuss the situations above. What would you have done?

"Actually, I don't think I would have done anything. I would have been annoyed, but . . ."

4 **Talk about it** True stories

Group work Take turns telling true stories about the situations below. Listen to your classmates and make suggestions. How should they have reacted? What could they have done differently?

Think about the last time you . . .

- ▸ weren't very polite.
- ▸ had an argument.
- ▸ hung up on someone.
- ▸ lost your temper.
- ▸ sulked or moped.
- ▸ made a complaint.

1 Building vocabulary

A Read the article. Do you agree or disagree with the statements? Check (✓) the boxes.

EMOTIONAL INTELLIGENCE

*Emotional **intelligence*** is the ability to manage your own and other people's emotions. Emotionally **intelligent** people can express their feelings clearly and appropriately, and they are generally optimistic and positive, with high self-esteem. Take the quiz and find out if you have high EQ. (Answer below.)

SELF-AWARENESS

	AGREE	DISAGREE
1. I'm **decisive**. I know what I want.	☐	☐
2. I'm not **impulsive**. I think before I act.	☐	☐
3. **Jealousy** is not part of my life. I am not a **jealous** person.	☐	☐

MANAGING EMOTIONS

	AGREE	DISAGREE
4. I don't feel **guilty** or **ashamed** about things I've done in the past.	☐	☐
5. **Aggressive** people don't **upset** me. I can cope with their **aggression**.	☐	☐
6. I don't get **angry** and **upset** if people disagree with me.	☐	☐

MOTIVATION

	AGREE	DISAGREE
7. I'm very **motivated**, and I set **realistic** goals for myself.	☐	☐
8. I have the **confidence**, **determination**, and **self-discipline** to achieve my goals.	☐	☐
9. My main **motivation** in life is to make others **happy**.	☐	☐

EMPATHY

	AGREE	DISAGREE
10. I know when my friends feel **sad** or **depressed**	☐	☐
11. I'm very **sympathetic** when a friend has a problem.	☐	☐
12. I think it's important to be **sensitive** to how other people are feeling.	☐	☐

SOCIAL SKILLS

	AGREE	DISAGREE
13. If friends want to do things I don't want to do, I try to be **flexible**.	☐	☐
14. I think it's good to express emotions like **grief**, **hate**, and **anger**, but in private.	☐	☐
15. **Honesty** is important to me. I'm **honest** with people unless it will upset them.	☐	☐

People with good EQ would agree with the statements above. The more Agree answers you gave, the higher your EQ score.

About you **B** Pair work Compare your answers. Are you alike? Give more information.

"I'm usually pretty decisive. It doesn't take me long to make decisions."

Word sort **C** Complete the chart with nouns and adjectives from the article. Then choose five words from the chart, and make true sentences about people you know to tell a partner.

noun	adjective	noun	adjective	noun	adjective
aggression	*aggressive*	guilt		realism	
	angry	happiness		sadness	
	confident	honesty			self-disciplined
depression			intelligent	sensitivity	
	determined	jealousy		shame	
flexibility			motivated	sympathy	

Vocabulary notebook p. 84

2 Building language

A ((•)) **3.13 Listen. What guesses do Paul and Ella make about why their friends are late?**

Paul   So, where are Alexis and Sam? Do you think they might have forgotten?

Ella   They couldn't have forgotten. I talked to Alexis just yesterday. They must have gotten tied up in traffic.

Paul   Or they might have had another one of their fights. Maybe Sam is off somewhere sulking, like the last time.

Ella   Either way, Alexis would have called us on her cell phone.

Paul   Well, she may not have remembered to take it with her. She forgets things when she's stressed out.

Ella   That's true. . . . Oh, guess what? My phone's dead! So she could have tried to call and not gotten through.

Paul   Oh, my gosh! The movie's about to start. We'd better go in.

Figure it out **B Can you think of some reasons why Alexis and Sam are late? Complete the sentences below. Use the conversation to help you.**

1. They must _____ .   2. They could _____ .   3. They may _____ .

3 Grammar Past modals for speculation ((•)) 3.14

Extra practice p. 147

> **You can use *must / could / may / might* + *have* + past participle to speculate about the past.**
>
> They **must have gotten** tied up in traffic.   = *I'm sure they got tied up in traffic.*
> She **could have tried** to call.   = *It's possible she tried to call.*
> They **may / might have had** a fight.   = *Maybe they had a fight.*
> She **may not / might not have remembered**. = *It's possible she didn't remember.*
> **Use *could not* + *have* + past participle to say what is not possible.**
> They **couldn't have forgotten**.   = *It's not possible they forgot.*

In conversation

Affirmative statements with past modals are much more common than negative statements.

A Imagine these situations. Complete the two possible explanations for each one.

⊗ Common errors

Use the past participle, not the base form of the verb.

*They could have **tried** to call.*
(NOT *They could have try to call.*)

1. One of your co-workers hasn't shown up for a meeting.
   She may _____ (forget), or she could _____ (get) tied up in another meeting.

2. You've sent your friend several text messages. She hasn't replied.
   She must _____ (not / receive) my messages. Her phone might _____ (die).

3. A friend promised to return a book he borrowed. He hasn't. He's normally very reliable.
   He could _____ (lose) it. On the other hand, he might _____ (not / finish) it yet.

4. A friend walked past you in the street and didn't stop to talk. She looked upset.
   She could _____ (not / see) you. She must _____ (have) something on her mind.

5. Your brother is supposed to drive you to the airport. He's already 20 minutes late.
   His car must _____ (break) down. Or he may _____ (not / remember).

B Pair work Think of two other explanations for each situation above. Discuss the possibilities.

((•· **Sounds right** p. 138

1 Conversation strategy   Sharing experiences

A Think of different ways to complete this sentence. Tell the class.

I get upset when people _____ on the subway.

B ◀)) 3.15 Listen. What annoys Mara and Hal?

Mara	Hey! That guy almost knocked you over getting off the elevator.
Hal	Yeah. He acted like we were in his way.
Mara	I get so annoyed with people like that.
Hal	Me too. Like, I get upset when people push on the subway. It's so rude.
Mara	Yeah, and speaking of rude people, how about the people who stand right in front of the subway doors and won't let you get off?
Hal	Oh, I had that happen to me just last night. These guys were like totally blocking the doors. And when I tried to get past them, they were like, "What's your problem?"
Mara	That reminds me of the time I got on the subway with my grandfather, and all these people pushed ahead of him to get seats.
Hal	Isn't he like 80 years old?
Mara	Yeah. I probably should have said something, but I didn't.

C **Notice** how Mara and Hal use expressions like these to share their experiences. Find examples in the conversation.

> I had that happen to me.   That reminds me (of) . . .
>
> That happened to me.   That's like . . .
>
> I had a similar experience.   Speaking of . . . ,

D Match the comments and responses. Then practice with a partner.

1. I hate it when you're going to park your car and someone takes your parking spot. _____

2. We went to this restaurant once. The waiter got our orders all wrong. He was terrible. _____

3. Don't you hate it when people start texting in the middle of a movie at the theater? _____

4. I was in line at an ATM last week, and this guy cut in line – he walked right in front of me. It was so rude. _____

a. Yeah. That's like when people are talking, and you miss something. It's so annoying.

b. I had that happen to me. This woman almost hit my car. I should have said something to her.

c. Speaking of rude people, I had a similar experience in the bank today. Someone pushed ahead of me.

d. That happened to me, so I complained. The manager just said sorry. We should have gotten a free dessert, at least!

About you **E** **Pair work** Do you agree with the people above? Have you had similar experiences? Discuss.

"I had that happen to me. Someone took my parking spot. They nearly hit my car."

2 Strategy plus *like*

You can use *like*...

To say something is similar.
He acted like we were in his way.

To highlight something.*
They were like totally blocking the doors.

To mean other things, including the verb *like*.

34%   5%   10%   18%   16%   17%

To say "approximately."*
Isn't he like 80 years old?

To report what someone said.*
They were like, "What's your problem?"

To give an example.
Like, I get upset ...

*Use in very informal conversations only.

In conversation

Like is one of the top 15 words. It is about six times more frequent in conversation than in writing.

🔊 **3.16 Read the comment below. Use *like* to replace the underlined words, and add other words you need. Then listen and check your answers.**

"One of my friends is kind of sensitive. ~~For example~~ *Like* , she thinks I'm criticizing her all the time when I'm just – how can I say this? – _____ trying to make a suggestion. She says, _____ , "Stop telling me what to do all the time." I guess I'm just more decisive than she is. I know I annoy her sometimes, but otherwise we get along really well. I guess we've been friends for about _____ ten years. It's funny. In other ways we're just the same as _____ each other."

3 Listening and strategies Similar experiences

A 🔊 **3.17 Listen to two people talk about their experiences with taxicabs. Number the incidents 1 to 5 in the order that they talk about them.**

☐ The cab driver wanted a tip.
☐ The cab driver scratched another vehicle.
☐ The cab driver nearly caused an accident.
☐ The cab driver got lost.
☐ The cab driver was having an argument on his phone.

B 🔊 **3.17 Listen again. Complete the sentences. Then answer the questions.**

1. The woman says, "I had a similar experience _____ ." What happened?
2. The man says, "That reminds me of the time I was taking a cab home _____ ." Why did the cab driver make rude comments?
3. The man says, "That's like when they _____ ." What example does he give?
4. The woman says, "I had that happen to me. The taxicab _____ ." What happened?

About you **C** **Pair work** Have you had any similar experiences with taxicabs? Discuss with a partner.

Free talk p. 133

1 Reading

A Think of a time when you apologized to someone. How did you do it? What advice do you have for someone making an apology? Make a list of "dos and don'ts."

"Don't wait too long."   *"Make sure your apology is sincere."*

B Read the article. Does the writer have any of the same advice?

APOLOGIES: THE KEY TO MAINTAINING FRIENDSHIPS

It's not always convenient or easy to say you're sorry. Sometimes we're too preoccupied to notice when we've hurt someone, or if we do, too busy to make a proper apology. In other cases, personal pride keeps us from admitting we've done something wrong. There are probably times when deep down we feel that we weren't entirely at fault, that the other person owes us an apology! Nevertheless, if we want to maintain good relationships with friends and colleagues, it's essential to know when and how to apologize:

1. _____ Even if it feels awkward to say you're sorry, do it as soon as possible. If you wait for the perfect moment, you may end up not apologizing at all. At the same time, if you've waited a bit too long, remember that it's never too late to say you're sorry and set things right.

2. _____ Don't let your personal pride get in the way of apologizing. Accept fully that you might have said or done something hurtful. Don't say, "I'm sorry if I offended anyone" or "I'm sorry you feel that way." This implies that you didn't really do anything wrong, that the other person is just overly sensitive. None of us is perfect, and there's no reason to feel embarrassed about needing to apologize.

3. _____ Our mistakes often have unpleasant consequences. An apology isn't complete unless you take responsibility both for hurting someone's feelings and for the specific problems you may have caused in that person's life.

4. _____ To show you're sincerely sorry, offer to repair any damage you've done. If you've broken something, offer to replace it. If you forgot a birthday, offer to take your friend out to dinner. Or if you're not sure what to do, say, "How can I make this up to you?"

5. _____ After admitting that you made a mistake, promise not to do it again, and keep to your commitment! If you have to apologize over and over for the same offenses, you'll soon lose the confidence of your friends.

Finally, sometimes we hesitate to say we're sorry because we feel the other person is more at fault and should apologize first! In these cases, remember that there are rights and wrongs on both sides of any conflict. Even if what happened wasn't 100 percent your fault, be the first to come forward and offer an apology. This act of kindness will make it clear just how much you value the other person's friendship. And it will make you feel better, too.

C Write the missing subheadings in the article.

a. Offer to make things right.

b. Apologize right away.

c. Promise to act differently in the future.

d. Acknowledge any damage caused.

e. Admit you did something wrong.

> **Reading tip**
>
> Read the subheadings in an article first to see what it covers.

D Find expressions in the article that are similar to the underlined expressions in the questions. Then ask and answer the questions with a partner.

1. Do you ever get so <u>busy thinking about something</u> that you forget to do things?
2. Have you ever said you were sorry, but <u>secretly in your mind</u> didn't mean it?
3. Can you think of any situations where it feels really <u>uncomfortable</u> to apologize?
4. What kinds of things <u>keep people from</u> apologizing?
5. Have you ever said to anyone, "How can I <u>compensate for this</u>?" What had you done?

2 Speaking and listening Good and bad apologies

A 🔊 **3.18** Listen to four conversations. Why is each person apologizing? Match the person to the reason. Write the letter. There is one extra reason.

1. Alex _____
2. Nora _____
3. Gregory _____
4. Adriana _____

a. forgot to meet a friend.
b. handed in an assignment late.
c. forgot someone's birthday.
d. offended a friend.
e. got into an argument.

B 🔊 **3.18** Listen again. Were the apologies effective? Give reasons. Complete the chart.

	Was it effective?	Why or why not?
1. Alex	Yes / No	_____
2. Nora	Yes / No	_____
3. Gregory	Yes / No	_____
4. Adriana	Yes / No	_____

About you **C** Pair work How would you apologize in the situations above? Discuss your ideas.

3 Writing A note of apology

A Read the email and the Help note. Underline the expressions Jason uses to apologize. Does his email follow the advice from the article on page 82?

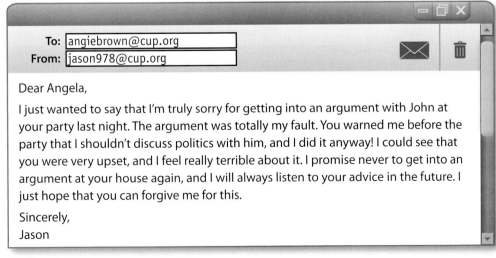

To: angiebrown@cup.org
From: jason978@cup.org

Dear Angela,

I just wanted to say that I'm truly sorry for getting into an argument with John at your party last night. The argument was totally my fault. You warned me before the party that I shouldn't discuss politics with him, and I did it anyway! I could see that you were very upset, and I feel really terrible about it. I promise never to get into an argument at your house again, and I will always listen to your advice in the future. I just hope that you can forgive me for this.

Sincerely,
Jason

Help note

Writing a note of apology
I just wanted to say I'm sorry for (not) _____ ing . . .
I would like to apologize for . . .
I feel I should apologize for . . .
I promise not to _____ again.
It was my fault entirely.

About you **B** Think of a time when you apologized or should have apologized to someone. Write an email to apologize. Then read your classmates' emails. Are the apologies effective?

83

Learning tip *Making connections*

When you learn new vocabulary, make a connection with something or someone you know. Think of how or when you would use the word or expression to talk about your life.

1 **Think of a person you know for each of the qualities below.**

1. _____ has a lot of self-confidence.
2. _____ is very good at controlling his or her anger.
3. _____ has no sympathy for people who complain a lot.
4. _____ has the motivation and determination to do well at work.

In conversation

Happy talk

People say *happy* more than they say *sad* or *unhappy*.

▇▇▇▇▇ *happy*
▇▇ *sad*
▪ *unhappy*

2 **Write a sentence for each adjective. Make a connection with a person or an experience.**

aggressive   flexible   impulsive   sensitive
depressed   guilty   jealous

My sister says she feels guilty when she eats too much chocolate.

3 **Word builder** Find and write the meaning of these expressions. Use words in Unit 8 to help you.

1. be / feel down in the dumps _____
2. be full of yourself _____
3. be / turn green with envy _____

4. be heartless _____
5. be set on doing something _____
6. go nuts / bananas _____

On your own

Do some people watching! The next time you are out and about, watch the people around you. Write notes when you get home.

He's getting really upset.

Can Do! Now I can . . .

✔ I can . . .   ❓ I need to review how to . . .

☐ talk about reactions and behavior.
☐ talk hypothetically about the past.
☐ describe emotions and personal qualities.
☐ speculate about the past.
☐ use expressions like *That reminds me (of)* to share experiences.

☐ use *like* in informal conversations.
☐ understand people sharing taxi experiences.
☐ understand a conversation about rude behavior.
☐ read an article on making apologies.
☐ write a note of apology.

Material world

✓ Can Do! In this unit, you learn how to . . .

Lesson A
- Talk about possessions and being materialistic
- Report things that people said

Lesson B
- Discuss money management
- Report questions that people asked

Lesson C
- Report the content of conversations
- Quote other people or sources of information

Lesson D
- Read a blog about decluttering
- Write a survey article about your classmates' possessions

Before you begin . . .

- What are your most important possessions?
- Is having a lot of possessions a good thing or bad thing?
- Do you think you are materialistic?

BUT IS IT ART?

British artist destroys his possessions.

"My goal is to destroy all my possessions. I have been making an inventory of everything I own, and it comes to 7,006 items, from televisions to reading material to records to old love letters to my Saab 900. These are the things I have accumulated in the 37 years of my life. Some of them are hard to part with, like my father's sheepskin coat, which he gave to me many years ago. But I have made a conceptual decision as an artist to shred and granulate everything."

". . . I am also destroying artwork – my own as well as some by my friends. They said it was OK. They understand my project. At the end of this week, after my possessions are turned into granules, I want to bury them underground in a shopping center. I haven't found the right shopping center yet."

A conveyor belt takes Michael Landy's possessions to a shredding machine.

1 Getting started

A What kind of art do you see around your town or city? Make a list. Do you like it?

"You see a lot of sculptures in the park. Some are interesting."

B Read what artist Michael Landy says about one of his projects. What is the project? Could you do the same thing with all your possessions?

C 3.19 Listen to Ginny talk about the article. Which facts didn't she get right? Do you agree with her opinion?

"I read about this British artist who came up with a really unusual art project. He said his goal was to destroy all his possessions and that he wanted to bury them in a parking lot! Can you believe it? He explained that he had been making a list of everything he owned and that it came to 17,000 items! And that he had made an artistic decision to shred and granulate everything. You can actually watch him destroying all his things. Someone explained to me that this is 'performance art.' I guess this guy really hates materialism. So do I, but I can't throw anything away. Just the same, maybe I'll stop buying so much stuff. . . . You know, I wonder why he didn't just give his stuff away. But I think it's a really interesting idea. I'd like to know more about this type of art."

Figure it out **D** Complete these sentences to report what Michael Landy said. Use Ginny's interview to help you.

1. Landy said his goal _____ to destroy all his possessions.
2. He explained some things _____ hard to part with.
3. He said his inventory _____ to 7,006 items.
4. He said he _____ a decision to bury them, but he _____ the right place yet.

2 Grammar Reported speech ◄)) 3.20

Extra practice p. 148

When you report the things people said, the verb tense often "shifts back."

Direct speech	Reported speech
Michael Landy:	He said (that) . . .
"My goal **is** to destroy all my possessions."	his goal **was** to destroy all his possessions.
"I **want** to bury them underground."	he **wanted** to bury them underground.
"My father **gave** me a sheepskin coat."	his father **had given** him a sheepskin coat.
"I **haven't found** the right shopping center."	he **hadn't found** the right shopping center.
"I **have been making** an inventory."	he **had been making** an inventory.
Ginny:	She said (that) . . .
"I **can't** throw anything away."	she **couldn't** throw anything away.
"Maybe I'**ll** stop buying so much stuff."	maybe she **would** stop buying so much stuff.

When you report information that is still true, the verb tense often remains the same.
Someone explained to me that this **is** what you call "performance art."

Here are some things people said about their possessions. Complete the sentences to report what they said. Compare with a partner. Do you know any people like these?

1. "I'm not at all materialistic – I have very few possessions."
   A friend of mine said that he _wasn't materialistic_ and that he ____had very few possessions____ .

2. "My closets are all full, but I can't stop buying new clothes."
   Someone at work told me that her closets _____ , but she _____ .

3. "I'm always throwing things away. Once I threw out an antique vase by mistake."
   My aunt said that she _____ and that once she _____ .

4. "We're in debt because we've spent too much money on stuff for our apartment."
   My brother told his wife that they _____ because they _____ .

5. "I have a huge collection of comic books that I just don't have room for."
   One of my teachers told me that he _____ .

6. "We'll have to have a yard sale to get rid of all the junk we've been buying at yard sales."
   My neighbors said they _____ .

7. "I never throw things away. I just leave things in the garage."
   Years ago, my cousin told me he _____ .

3 Speaking and listening Who's materialistic?

About you **A** **Pair work** Discuss the questions. How materialistic are you?

1. Do you like to have all the latest gadgets?
2. How thrifty are you? Are you careful with money?
3. Are you very attached to your possessions?
4. Have you ever gotten upset because you lost or broke something valuable?
5. Do you often buy things you don't need?

B ◄)) 3.21 Listen to Howard answer the questions above. Take notes on one thing he says in answer to each question. Then compare with a partner. How much detail can you remember?

"Howard said that he wasn't really interested in gadgets at all."

1 Building vocabulary

A 🔊 3.22 Listen and read the questionnaire from a money magazine. What kind of money manager are you?

What kind of money manager are you?

Go through our checklist to find out. Tally your answers and read your profile.

	Yes	No
1. Do you have a **monthly budget** and **stick to** it?	☐	☐
2. Do you **keep track of** how much you spend each week?	☐	☐
3. Do you give yourself an **allowance** for special "treats"?	☐	☐
4. Do you **pay** all your **bills** on time?	☐	☐
5. Do you **set aside money** each month in a **savings account**?	☐	☐
6. Do you have a bank account that **pays** good **interest**?	☐	☐
7. Do you **invest money in** reliable **stocks** and **bonds**?	☐	☐
8. Have you **put** enough **money away** for "a rainy day"?	☐	☐
9. Do you **pay in cash** or **by check** to avoid **charging** too much to a **credit card**?	☐	☐
10. When you borrow money from friends or family, do you **pay** it **back** right away?	☐	☐
11. If you **took out** a **loan**, would you **pay** it **off** as soon as you could?	☐	☐
12. If you **got into debt**, would you know how to **get out of debt**?	☐	☐

0-6 Yes answers: You're relaxed about managing your money. You're not worried about how much money you have, but you might need to do something to get things under control.

7-12 Yes answers: You're very systematic and careful with your money. Managing your money is important to you. You might need to make sure it doesn't make you feel stressed.

B Pair work What are your money habits? Complete the chart with sentences. Use ideas from the questionnaire, and add your own. Compare with a partner.

I ...	I don't ...
have a monthly budget.	*invest money in stocks.*

"I have a monthly budget, but I don't always stick to it."

Vocabulary notebook p. 94

2 Building language

A 🔊 **3.23** Listen. What did the market researcher ask John? Practice the conversation.

John   I was stopped by one of those market researchers today. She was doing a survey on money.

Mother   Really? What kind of things was she asking?

John   She wanted to know whether I was a spender or a saver and how I usually paid for things.

Mother   Hmm. Did you tell her I pay for everything?

John   Uh, no. . . . Anyway, then she asked me how many times I'd used a credit card in the past month. I told her I didn't have one, and the next thing I knew, she asked if I wanted to apply for one!

Mother   But you're only 18!

John   Well, I filled out the application anyway. The only thing is, . . . she asked if a parent could sign it, so . . .

Figure it out **B** How would John report these questions? Write sentences starting with *She asked me* . . .

1. Are you a regular saver?
2. Do you want a credit card?
3. How many times have you spent too much?
4. Can you sign this form?

3 Grammar   Reported questions 🔊 **3.24**

Extra practice p. 148

Direct questions	Reported questions
The market researcher:	She asked (me) . . . / She wanted to know . . .
"**Are** you a spender or a saver?"	if / whether I **was** a spender or a saver.
"How **do** you usually **pay** for things?"	how I usually **paid** for things.
"How many times **have** you **used** a credit card?"	how many times I**'d used** a credit card.
"**Can** one of your parents **sign** the application?"	if / whether one of my parents **could sign** it.

A Imagine the market researcher asked you these questions. Write reported questions.

❌ Common errors

Use statement word order in reported questions.

She asked how I usually paid for things.
(NOT *She asked how ~~did I usually pay~~ for things.*)

1. "What is your main source of income?"

    She asked me what my main source of income was.

2. "Are you relaxed about spending money?"

3. "Do you usually pay in cash, or do you often charge things to a credit card?"

4. "Can you stick to a monthly budget?"

5. "Have you taken anything back to a store recently?"

6. "How many times have you borrowed money from friends or family?"

7. "How much money can you spend on treats each month?"

8. "Do you have any loans? Are you paying them off as soon as you can?"

About you **B** **Pair work** Take turns reporting the questions and giving your answers.

"She asked me what my main source of income was, and I told her it was my parents!"

((• Sounds right p. 139

1 Conversation strategy Reporting the content of a conversation

A Do you agree with the saying, "Money can't buy happiness"? Tell the class.

B 🔊 3.25 Listen. What does Lucy know about Jeff and Lee?

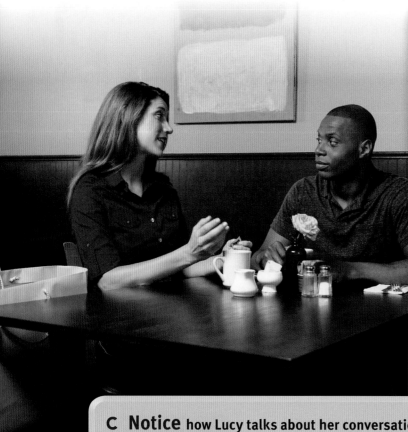

Lucy	I ran into Max last week. He was telling me that Jeff and Lee aren't getting along that well. They've only been married six months. Apparently, they're having money problems.
Omar	But I heard they're pretty wealthy. Or so someone was telling me.
Lucy	Yeah, well, evidently the honeymoon and the diamond ring and everything were all paid for on credit cards. Max was telling me that Lee had no idea they were in debt.
Omar	Really? How could she *not* know? There's got to be something wrong, you know, if she had no idea what was going on.
Lucy	Yeah, that's what Max was saying. He went to see them, and he was saying how much stuff they have in their house. But as he said, "Money can't buy happiness."
Omar	Obviously not.

C Notice how Lucy talks about her conversation with Max. She uses past continuous reporting verbs to focus on the content rather than the actual words she heard. Also, she generally doesn't "shift" tenses. Find examples.

"Max was telling me that Jeff and Lee aren't getting along that well."

D Imagine people you know said the things below. Rewrite the sentences to report what they said. Use past continuous reporting verbs.

1. A friend of yours: "I'm saving up to buy a car. I want a little two-seater sports car."
   A friend of mine was telling me she's saving up to buy a car. She was saying . . .
2. Your classmate: "My fiancée and I are going to have a small wedding. We decided big weddings are a waste of money. We'd rather have a nice honeymoon, so we've set aside some money for a trip to Sydney."
3. Your neighbors: "We want to put in a new kitchen, but we're going to have to take out a loan to pay for it. It's expensive."
4. Your co-worker: "I'm thinking of leaving my job and going back to school. I want to become a teacher. I think I'll be happier in that kind of a job than I am now."

About you **E Pair work** What have people told you recently? Tell a partner.

2 Strategy plus Quoting information

**When you quote information you've heard,
use these expressions to identify the source:**
Max was telling me / was saying / told me . . .
(As) he said, " . . . " According to Max, . . .

Use these when you don't identify the source:
Apparently, . . . Evidently, . . .
I was told . . . I('ve) heard . . .
They say . . . I('ve) read . . .

Apparently, they're having money problems.

As he said, "Money can't buy happiness."

Pair work Discuss the questions. Use the expressions above in your answers to talk about what you've heard or read.

1. Who's the richest person in the world?
2. What's a good way to invest money?
3. What's the best way to set money aside for college?
4. What's the quickest way to make a million dollars?
5. Which businesses have been successful in your city?
6. What's the most expensive thing you think you'll ever buy?
7. What's the best way to keep track of your spending?
8. Which jobs pay the best salaries? the worst?
9. Where's a good place to get a part-time job?

A Isn't it Carlos Slim Helú? I've heard he's worth billions.
B Yeah. My friend was telling me there are a lot of billionaires in Mexico now.

3 Speaking naturally Finished and unfinished ideas

	Finished idea:	**Unfinished idea:**
Sue was telling me about her job.	*It pays really well.* ⤸	*It pays really well . . .* ⤸

A ◀)) 3.26 Listen and repeat the sentences above. Notice how the intonation falls to show the speaker has finished an idea and rises to show there's more to say.

B ◀)) 3.27 Listen. Which of these sentences are finished ideas (F)? Which sound unfinished (U)? Write *F* or *U*.

1. Dan was telling me about his new career ＿＿＿
2. Evidently he's quit his job ＿＿＿
3. He has no other source of income ＿＿＿
4. He's trying to sell his art online ＿＿＿
5. It all seems a little risky to me ＿＿＿
6. I hope it pays off for him in the end ＿＿＿

C ◀)) 3.28 Now listen to the full extract, and check your answers. Do you think Dan's situation is risky?

About you **D** **Group work** What are some good ways to make money? Which jobs pay well? Which don't? Tell your group about things you've heard and read.

"My sister was telling me her boyfriend is a stockbroker. Apparently, he makes a fortune."

1 Reading

A Have you ever bought things that you don't use? What are they? Tell the class.

B Read the article. What was Leda's problem? What did she do about it?

> **Reading tip**
>
> Journalistic feature articles and blogs sometimes pretend to "speak" to the reader, e.g., *You know what?* Don't do this in academic writing.

---

http://www.leda...

ABOUT ME   FASHION & BEAUTY   **HOME & DESIGN**   FOOD & DRINK   TRAVEL   CONTACT ME   FAQS   PHOTO GALLERY   OLDER POSTS

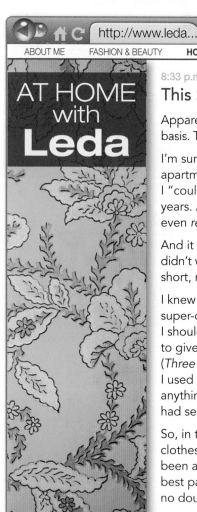

AT HOME with **Leda**

8:33 p.m. September 26

This Stuff's Gotta Go!

Apparently, we only use 20 percent of the stuff we own on a regular basis. The rest just sits in our drawers and closets, cluttering up our lives.

I'm sure that's true in my case. As of last month, every corner of my apartment was crammed with cardboard boxes, full of junk that I "could never live without." Most of those boxes I hadn't opened in years. And you know what? I hadn't missed any of it. Actually, I didn't even *remember* what was in those boxes.

And it wasn't just the boxes. I had closets overflowing with clothes I didn't wear, books I was attached to but never read, old electronics that no longer worked – in short, my home was full of clutter, and I didn't have room for it all.

I knew I had to get things under control, so I called up my friend Willow. You know, that super-organized, less-is-more kind of friend that many of us have? Yeah, her. She said that I should go through all of my belongings and make an inventory. She then told me I needed to give away or sell anything I had more than one of . . . like the *three* coffee pots I had. (*Three* coffee pots? How did I even *get* three coffee pots?) Finally, Willow asked me how often I used my things. She explained that she keeps her home clutter-free by getting rid of anything that she hasn't worn or used in the last year. She added that I could keep things that had sentimental value, as long as they were *really* important and special.

So, in the past month, I've gotten rid of more than TWENTY boxes of junk and bags of clothes. Some of it I donated, recycled, or trashed, but most of it I sold. Decluttering has been an enormous task, but it has felt great to reclaim the space in my home again. And the best part? The cash I earned helped me pay off my credit card debt – something I had, no doubt, because I had bought too much stuff in the first place. ☺

C Read the article again. Are these sentences true or false? Check (✓) the boxes. Find the sentences in the article that support your answers.

		True	False
1.	The writer says people use most of their things on a regular basis.	☐	☐
2.	She used to think she needed most of the things in her boxes.	☐	☐
3.	She had plenty of space in her closet for her clothes.	☐	☐
4.	The writer's friend, Willow, told her to make a list of her belongings.	☐	☐
5.	Willow told her to keep one thing out of each box.	☐	☐
6.	Willow believes you should only keep things you use and need.	☐	☐
7.	The writer found decluttering difficult but is happy that she has done it.	☐	☐
8.	The writer solved another problem with the money she made from selling her stuff.	☐	☐

^{About}_{you} **D** Find expressions in the article to replace the underlined expressions below. Then ask and answer the questions with a partner.

1. Do you think you use only 20 percent of your things <u>regularly</u>?
2. Do you have closets that are <u>full of</u> things you don't need?
3. Which of your possessions are you <u>especially fond of</u>?
4. Could you get rid of anything that has <u>a deep, emotional meaning</u> for you?
5. Have you ever tried to <u>get rid of things you don't want in</u> your home? Was it a big <u>job</u>?

2 Listening and writing I couldn't live without . . .

A ◀)) 3.29 Listen to four people talk about things they couldn't live without. What do they talk about? Why couldn't they live without these things? Complete the chart.

	He / She couldn't live without . . .	because . . .
1. Bruno		
2. Diana		
3. Midori		
4. Max		

^{About}_{you} **B** ◀)) 3.30 Listen again to the opinions. Do you agree? Write a response to each person.

1. _____
2. _____
3. _____
4. _____

C **Class activity** Ask your classmates, "What's one thing you couldn't live without? Why?" Take notes on three interesting ideas.

D Read the Help note and the article below. Underline the verbs used for reporting speech. Then write an article about your classmates. Use both direct speech and reported speech.

Things my classmates couldn't live without

One of my classmates, Mieko, said she couldn't live without her violin. "It's my most valuable possession," she explained. She got her first violin at the age of six. "I was so excited," she recalled. She took lessons in school and practiced every day. She is now an accomplished violinist. "I couldn't live without it," she concluded.

 Help note

Reporting verbs for direct and reported speech
- Saying and explaining:
  "It's valuable," she **said / told me / explained**.
  *She **said / told me / explained** that it was valuable.*
- Remembering:
  "I lost it once," she **remembered / recalled**.
  *She **remembered / recalled** that she had lost it once.*
- Adding and finishing:
  "I love my violin," she **added / concluded**.
  *She **added / concluded** that she loved her violin.*

E Read a classmate's article. Then tell the class about something one of your classmates couldn't live without. Which thing is the most interesting or unusual?

Free talk p. 134

Learning tip *Collocations*

When you learn a new word, notice its *collocations* – the words that are used with it. In this example, *open* and *close a bank account* are collocations.

bank account: You can open and close a bank account.

1 Cross out the words that are *not* collocations of the verbs below.

make	a credit card / a budget / a living
apply for	a job / a credit card / a bill
open	a savings account / a restaurant / a debt
pay off	a debt / a budget / a loan
invest in	loans / bonds / stocks

2 Write collocations for these words and expressions. How many ideas can you think of?

Find verbs for these nouns

an allowance	cash
a bank account	a discount
a bill	money
a budget	

Find adjectives for these nouns

allowance	expense
account	job
a budget	

earn / make / spend money

3 **Word builder** Find the meanings of the words and expressions below. Use them in a sentence.

credit limit   due date   interest rate   nest egg   overdrawn account

On your own

Make a wish list of your financial goals. What would you like to accomplish in the next 5 years? 10 years? 20 years?

I'd like to buy a car in 5 years.
I'd like to buy a house in 10 years.

✓ Can Do! Now I can . . .

✓ I can . . .   ? I need to review how to . . .

- ☐ talk about possessions and materialism.
- ☐ discuss money management.
- ☐ report things that people said.
- ☐ report questions that people asked.
- ☐ report the content of conversations I've had.
- ☐ quote other people or sources of information.

- ☐ understand an interview about possessions.
- ☐ understand people talking about what they couldn't live without.
- ☐ read a blog about decluttering.
- ☐ write a survey article about my classmates' possessions.

1 What would you have done?

A Complete the story using the correct forms of the verbs and expressions in the box.

apply for a credit card	get out of debt	invest money in	pay good interest	set aside money
✓ get an allowance	have a budget	keep track of	pay in cash	take out a loan

When Andrew was growing up, he was careful with his money. He _got an allowance_ every week from his parents, and because he wanted to go to college, he _____ every month. He opened a savings account that _____ , so his savings grew. When he started college, he didn't have much money, but he _____ and stuck to it. He _____ the money he spent, and when he bought things, he always _____ .

But then, Andrew won $1 million in a lottery, and everything changed. He didn't _____ stocks and bonds. Instead, he went on a spending spree. He bought a house, a car, designer clothes, and a laptop, and he spent a lot on travel and entertainment. Soon he had nothing left, so he _____ and started charging his everyday expenses. To pay his college tuition fees, he _____ , which he is still paying off. Andrew graduated from college and has a good job now, but he still hasn't _____ .

B Answer the questions using past modals *would have*, *should have*, *could have*, *must have*, *might have*, or *may have*. Discuss your answers with a partner.

1. What should Andrew have done with the money he won?
2. Is there anything he shouldn't have done?
3. What would you have done differently? What wouldn't you have done?
4. How do you think he must have felt after he'd spent all the money?
5. Why do you think Andrew went on a spending spree?

C **Pair work** Take turns retelling Andrew's story. Use the expressions *Apparently*, *Evidently*, and *I heard that*. Does it remind you of similar stories? Share them using *That reminds me* or *That's like*.

2 How many words can you remember?

Complete the charts. How many words can you think of to describe personal qualities or emotions? Compare with a partner. Then ask and answer questions using words from your charts.

Nouns	Adjectives
honesty	happy

"Is honesty important to you?"   *"Are you generally a happy person?"*

3 So what were they saying?

A Complete these quotations with a problem and then add a solution, using the appropriate form of the verb given.

1. John: "I went rock climbing, and I got this really big _hole / tear_ in my backpack. It needs _to be sewn / sewing_ (sew). Are you good at sewing?"

2. Alice: "My kitchen faucet keeps _____ , and I can't turn it off. It needs _____ (fix), but I can't afford to get a plumber _____ (do) it right now. Can you take a look at it?"

3. Robert: "I have this big oil _____ on my good jacket. I have to have it _____ (clean) before my job interview next week. Which dry cleaner's has the fastest service?"

4. Maria: "My watch has been running _____ . I've never had the battery _____ (change), so it probably needs _____ (replace). How much will a new battery cost?"

5. Hilary: "I had a car accident, and one of my doors got a big _____ in it. I've been looking for a place to get it _____ (fix). Who fixed your car after your accident?"

B Report the general content of each person's problem, using *was saying (that)* or *was telling me (that)*. Then report exactly what the person said and asked about the solution, shifting the tenses back.

"John was saying that he got a hole in his backpack when he went rock climbing. He said that it needed to be sewn, and then he asked if I was good at sewing!"

4 Want some help?

A Complete the conversations with words like *Yuck, Ow, Ouch, Oops, Ooh, Ugh, Uh-oh*, and *Shoot*. Sometimes more than one answer is possible. Then practice with a partner.

1. A ___Ow!___ I just got an electric shock. I should get that iron fixed.
   B _____ I bet that hurt. Are you OK?

2. A _____ My computer just crashed again. I can't understand it. It keeps happening.
   B _____ Maybe you have a virus. Do you want me to look at it?

3. A _____ I'm hungry. Do you want a snack?
   B Sure. Let's see. Do you want some scrambled eggs?
   A _____ I can't stand eggs.
   B _____ I just dropped them. Oh, well, never mind.

4. A _____ I forgot to hand in my homework today.
   B _____ Will your teacher be mad?
   A Probably. _____ look, it's all messed up. And oh _____ . There's chewing gum stuck to it.

B Pair work Make each sentence shorter if possible, and practice again. Can you continue the conversations?

A Ow! Just got a shock. I should get that fixed.

B Ouch! Bet that hurt. You OK?

A Yeah. Think so. Guess I ought to . . .

Fame

✓ Can Do! In this unit, you learn how to . . .

Lesson A
- Talk about celebrities' rise to fame
- Use *if* clauses to say how things might have been different

Lesson B
- Talk about achieving and losing fame
- Use tag questions to give opinions or check information

Lesson C
- Use tag questions to soften advice and give encouragement
- Answer difficult questions with expressions like *It's hard to say*

Lesson D
- Read an article about child stars
- Write a profile of a successful person

1 Duke and Duchess of Cambridge

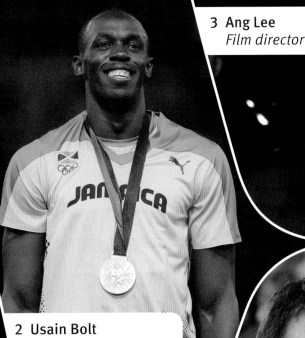

2 Usain Bolt
Olympic gold medalist

3 Ang Lee
Film director

5 Javier Bardem
Actor

4 J.K. Rowling
Author

Before you begin . . .

- What are some ways that people become famous?
- What do you think is the best thing about being famous?
- What is the worst thing about being famous?

http://www.watsoninfo...

A lucky break

Russell Watson's rise to fame was remarkable and unexpected. The English-born tenor had no formal music training, was an average student, and quit school at 16 to work in a factory. To make extra money, he sang in pubs in his spare time. Several years later, he sang in a radio talent contest and won, and his life took an amazing turn. He quit his job, got a manager, and started singing in clubs full-time. One night he ended a set of pop songs with an aria from an opera and got a standing ovation. He realized he was on to something. That's how he became a famous singer. By the age of 28, he had released his first album, *The Voice*, and had become an international star.

Comments

Dennis

I think it's a good thing he entered that contest. If he hadn't won, he might not have had the confidence to become a singer. And what would have happened if he had stayed in school? Maybe he would have done something entirely different.

Stephanie

Well, it's hard to know for certain, but I think he would have found a way to be a singer anyway. In fact, if he had continued his education, he could have had formal training and gotten an earlier start as a singer.

Anne

You might be right, Stephanie, but it was pretty brave of him to quit his job. If he hadn't quit and gotten a manager, he might not have had a singing career at all. What amazes me, though, is that he had enough nerve to sing something from an opera in a club! If he had only sung pop songs, he wouldn't have realized how much people loved his opera voice.

1 Getting started

A What kinds of talent contests can you enter? Would you enter one?

B Read the article "A lucky break" above. How did Russell Watson get his start as a professional singer?

C 4.01 Listen to the comments that people posted on the website about Russell Watson's career. Which comments do you agree with?

Figure it out **D** Can you complete the sentences below? Compare with a partner.

1. If Russell Watson had stayed in school, maybe he _____ had a very different career.

2. If he _____ won that talent contest, he might not have become a singer.

3. If he had only sung pop songs, he _____ known people loved his opera voice.

4. What _____ happened if he had only sung pop songs?

Grammar Talking hypothetically about the past 🔊)) 4.02

Extra practice p. 149

You can use sentences with *if* to talk hypothetically about the past.
Use the past perfect form in the *if* clause and a past modal in the main clause.

If + past perfect	Past modal *would have, could have, might have*, etc.
If Watson **had stayed** in school,	maybe he **would have done** something entirely different.
If he **hadn't won** the talent contest,	he **might not have had** the confidence to become a singer.
If he **had continued** his education,	he **could have gotten** formal music training.

Hypothetical questions about the past
What **would have happened** if he **had stayed** in school?
What **would** he **have done** if he **hadn't won** the talent contest?
Would he **have become** a singer?

In conversation

People often say *If I would have* instead of *If I had*, but this is not considered correct in writing.

✗ Common errors

Use *if* + past perfect, not simple past.

If he **hadn't quit** his job, he wouldn't have become a singer.
(NOT If he ~~didn't quit~~ his job . . .)

A Read the extract about a woman who became famous through the Internet.
Then complete the sentences using the verbs given.

Rebecca Black became an online sensation when her mother paid a record company to produce a music video of her daughter singing a song called "Friday." The video was uploaded onto a video-sharing website and watched by millions of people. Many music critics and viewers didn't like it, and some people called it "the worst song ever." Black appeared on several talk shows, and "Friday" soon became the most-watched video of the year. Black became a "viral star" and is now a successful artist.

1. If Rebecca's mother ___hadn't paid___ (not pay) the record company, they _wouldn't have produced_ (not produce) the video, and they _____ (not upload) it.

2. If the record company _____ (not upload) the video, millions of people _____ (not watch) it, and Rebecca _____ (might not become) a viral star.

3. What _____ (happen) if the song _____ (got) good reviews? _____ Black _____ (become) famous if more people _____ (like) the song? It's hard to tell, but it _____ (might receive) less media attention.

4. If Black _____ (not have) all the bad publicity, her music career _____ (might not take) off. She _____ (miss) out if she _____ (listen) to all the critics.

About you **B** Write about two things that have happened to you. Use the ideas below or your own. How would your life have been different if these things hadn't happened?

a job you got	a person you met	something fun that happened to you	a trip you took

Getting my current job is one of the best things that has happened to me. If my friend hadn't told me about the job, I wouldn't have gotten it. If I had stayed in my old job, . . .

C **Pair work** Take turns talking about each situation. Ask your partner questions for more information.

1 Building vocabulary and grammar

A 🔊 **4.03** Listen. How did Lana become famous? Practice the conversation.

Jon   Look. Lana's at the Swan Club! You haven't seen her show yet, have you?

Kylie   No, but I'd love to go. . . . She's a blues singer, isn't she?

Jon   Actually, she's an **up-and-coming** rock star. She's been **in the headlines** a lot recently.

Kylie   Really? I guess I'm a little out of touch, aren't I?

Jon   She was on that talent show, and since then, her **career**'s really **taken off**.

Kylie   Oh, I know who she is! She won the show this year, didn't she?

Jon   Yeah, she did. Last year she was a student, and now she's **making headlines** as a rock singer. It's amazing, isn't it?

Kylie   Huh. She must have **had connections**.

Jon   I don't think so. She **got discovered** in a karaoke club by one of the show's producers. She was just **in the right place at the right time**.

Kylie   I wonder what happened to the guy who won last year – Java Thomas. He's kind of **dropped out of sight**, hasn't he?

Jon   Well, he **got** a lot of **bad press** when he got caught shoplifting.

Kylie   Shoplifting? That wasn't too smart, was it?

Jon   No, it wasn't, and his **career** has really **gone downhill**.

Word sort **B** Complete the chart using expressions in the conversation. Then tell a partner about someone famous. What do you know about him or her?

Ways to become famous	When you're becoming famous	When things don't work out
You get _discovered_ by someone.	Your career _____ .	Your career _____ .
You're just in _____ .	You make _____ .	You get bad _____ .
You have _____ .	You're _____ a lot.	You _____ of sight.
	You're an _____ star.	

Vocabulary notebook p. 106

Figure it out **C** How would Jon and Kylie make these statements into questions?

1. Lana's a singer, _____ ?

2. She won a talent show, _____ ?

3. Java Thomas wasn't too smart, _____ ?

4. His career hasn't taken off, _____ ?

2 Speaking naturally Intonation of tag questions

You're not sure and want to check something:	You're sure and think someone will agree:
You haven't seen her show yet, have you?	It's amazing, isn't it?

🔊 **4.04** Listen and repeat the questions above. Notice how the intonation rises or falls depending on the purpose of the question. Then practice Jon and Kylie's conversation again.

3 Grammar Tag questions 🔊 4.05

Extra practice p. 149

> Tag questions are statements followed by short questions in the same tense, called "tags."
>
> **Affirmative statement + negative tag**
> It's amazing, **isn't it?**
> That was a dumb thing to do, **wasn't it?**
> She won the talent show, **didn't she?**
> He's dropped out of sight, **hasn't he?**
>
> **Answer *yes* to agree.**
> She won the talent show, **didn't she?**
>   Yes, she did.
>
> **Negative statement + affirmative tag**
> It's not easy to become famous, **is it?**
> That wasn't too smart, **was it?**
> She didn't have connections, **did she?**
> His career hasn't taken off, **has it?**
>
> **Answer *no* to agree.**
> That wasn't too smart, **was it?**
>   No, it wasn't.

> 📧 **In conversation**
> Negative tags are much more frequent than affirmative tags.

A Complete the conversations with tag questions.

1. A You've heard of Chris Martin, _____ ?

   B I think so. He sings with Coldplay, _____ ?

   A Yeah. He's their lead singer.

   B Right. They're not American, _____ ?

   A No, they're British. I love their music. They're a great band, _____ ?

   B Oh, yeah. They've raised a lot of money for charity, too, _____ ? I mean, they do a lot of charity concerts and stuff, _____ ?

   A Yeah. I went to one. It was amazing.

2. A When was Marilyn Monroe famous? It was in the 1950s, _____ ?

   B Yeah, but she made a movie in the 1960s, too, _____ ?

   A I think you're right. She was mainly a movie star, _____ ? I mean, she wasn't a singer, _____ ?

   B Well, she sang in some of her movies, but she was basically an actress. You've seen her movies, _____ ?

   A No, but I'd like to. It's amazing, _____ ? She died years ago, but she's still famous.

B **Pair work** How would *you* say the tags above: with rising intonation (you're checking), or with falling intonation (you think your partner will agree)? Practice the conversations.

4 Talk about it Who's hot? Who's not?

Group work Discuss the questions. Who knows the most about people in the news?

▸ Where do you find out the latest celebrity news?

▸ Who's in the headlines these days? Why? Is anyone getting bad press?

▸ Who are the up-and-coming celebrities right now? Whose careers have taken off recently? Why?

▸ Can you think of any stars who have dropped out of sight? Why do you think their careers went downhill?

🔊 **Sounds right** p. 139

1 **Conversation strategy** Giving encouraging advice

A What advice would you give a friend who is not learning much from a class? Make a list of ideas.

B 🔊 4.06 Listen. What is Nela's problem, and what is Steve's advice?

Steve	So, how's your acting class going?
Nela	It's hard to say. It's fun, but I'm not learning much.
Steve	Well, you could look for another class, couldn't you?
Nela	Maybe. The thing is, I like the teacher, but she hardly notices me. She never gives me any feedback.
Steve	Hmm. How can you get her attention?
Nela	Good question. I wish I knew. Actually, I'm thinking of dropping out.
Steve	Well, before you do that, it would be good to talk with her, wouldn't it?
Nela	I'm not sure I want to know what she thinks! I mean, most of the other students have been acting since they were kids. Do you think that if I'd gotten an earlier start, I'd be a better actor by now?
Steve	That's a tough one. I don't know. But you've only been in the class a few weeks. You should at least give it a chance, shouldn't you?
Nela	You're right. I guess I should.

C **Notice** how Steve uses tag questions to soften his advice and give Nela encouragement. Find examples in the conversation.

"You could look for another class, couldn't you?"

D Match the problems and advice. Then role-play the conversations, and take turns giving your own advice.

1. I'd really like to record my own podcast. But I'm not sure what topic to choose. _____

2. I really want to be a contestant on one of those TV game shows. But I'm not sure what kind of people they're looking for. _____

3. If I'd had formal training when I was young, I think I could have been a singer. _____

4. I'd like to act in a college play, but I get scared when I perform in front of people. _____

a. Well, it's never too late. You could still get voice lessons now, couldn't you?

b. It would help if you just practiced speaking out loud at home, wouldn't it? That might help with stage fright.

c. Well, you should pick something you know about, shouldn't you? Or something that interests you.

d. You could just look online, couldn't you? Though I bet they want confident people. Or people with a sense of humor.

2 Strategy plus *It's hard to say.*

You can use expressions like these when a question is difficult to answer.

It's hard to say.
(That's a) Good question.
That's a tough one.

How can you get her attention? | Good question. I wish I knew.

About you | **Pair work** Ask and answer the questions. Use the expressions above if the question is difficult.

1. Would you like to be famous? Why or why not?
2. How would being famous change your lifestyle?
3. Do you think being famous would change you as a person? How?
4. If you became famous, would you keep all of your old friends?
5. They say everyone gets 15 minutes of fame. What would you like to be famous for?
6. What would you have done if you hadn't continued your education?

A *Would you like to be famous?*
B *Well, good question. I mean, it could be exciting. But I think I'd get tired of all the attention.*

3 Listening and strategies *Great advice*

A 🔊 **4.07** Look at some advice for making a band successful. What else could you do? Then listen to Tom talk to George about his band. Check (✓) the things Tom needs to do.

☐ practice more
☐ write more new songs
☐ play more "gigs"
☐ contact the local radio station

☐ record music and put it online
☐ get a manager
☐ choose a catchy name for the band

B 🔊 **4.07** Listen again. Answer the questions. Circle *a* or *b*.

1. What kinds of songs does the band play?
   a. their own original songs   b. other bands' songs
2. Where have they played?
   a. at local colleges   b. at one or two big clubs
3. What does George think about getting the band's name known?
   a. He says it's hard.   b. He thinks it's easy.
4. What does Tom think of his band's name?
   a. It's a cool name.   b. He doesn't really like it.

About you | **C** Imagine you want to become famous. Choose an idea below or think of your own. What would you like to achieve? What problems would you face? Make a list.

become an athlete   start a band   go on a TV show   create a popular blog

D **Pair work** Discuss your ideas. Take turns giving advice.

A *Actually, I already write a blog, but I would like to get a wider audience. How do you do that?*
B *Well, that's a tough one. It would help if you added some useful links to your blog, wouldn't it?*

1 Reading

A Can you think of any child stars? How do you think their lives are different from other children's lives?

B Read the magazine article. What is "Child Star Syndrome"? How have some actors coped with it?

> **Reading tip**
>
> Writers often use words like *some*, *others*, and *many* to avoid repeating the same noun (e.g., child actors).

Three Child Stars Who Beat the Odds

"Child Star Syndrome"

So many former child actors reach their teens and end up in the headlines as they lose control of their lives. Some face pressure from parents and spend their early years working long hours, trying to achieve stardom. Others are unable to manage all the money, attention, and the glamorous lifestyle as they get older. Many simply find it difficult to grow up under the scrutiny of the media, and as they become adults, their careers often go downhill, or they eventually drop out of sight. However, not all child stars fail under the pressures of fame. Some have shown that it *is* possible to balance an acting career with a normal life.

Natalie Portman: In the Right Place at the Right Time

Actress Natalie Portman was 11 when she got discovered by an agent in a pizza shop. She became well known for her role in the *Star Wars* series beginning in 1999. The support of Portman's parents helped keep her life stable. They encouraged her to concentrate on her education even when she was traveling and filming. She even skipped the premiere of her first blockbuster movie to study for high school exams. In 2000, Portman took time off from acting to focus on her studies, and in 2003, she received a degree in psychology from Harvard University. After graduation, she starred in several movies, and in 2010, she won an Academy Award for her performance in the movie *Black Swan*. She admits that nothing is more important than her family life.

The Talented Young Stars of *Harry Potter*

English-born Daniel Radcliffe and Emma Watson were barely 11 years old when they began acting in the world-famous *Harry Potter* series in 2001. Fame and fortune certainly changed their lives, but with the support of their families (their parents were never impressed by fame) and the other actors on the set, they had healthy childhoods. Both Watson and Radcliffe earned excellent grades in school, and Watson was accepted into Brown University in Rhode Island and later Oxford University. As young adults, neither of them was interested in the glamorous lifestyle that their wealth would allow them to have. Their down-to-earth attitude hasn't stopped their ambitions, though. Both have secured leading roles in movies and the theater.

What's Their Secret?

If these actors hadn't had the support of parents and other adults, and if they hadn't had a high level of maturity, strength, and confidence, they might not have become the successful adult actors they are today. They've managed to cope extraordinarily well with the pressures of fame – a great achievement when you consider what could have gone wrong in their young lives.

C Find words and expressions in the article to replace the underlined words in the questions. Then ask and answer the questions with a partner.

1. What can happen to child actors who grow up <u>in the public eye</u>?
2. Is it possible to <u>combine</u> an acting career with an education?
3. What <u>very successful</u> movies has Natalie Portman starred in?
4. What did Portman decide to <u>concentrate</u> on in 2000?
5. How old were the *Harry Potter* stars when filming began – 10, or <u>only just</u> 11?
6. What types of <u>parts</u> have Daniel Radcliffe and Emma Watson <u>managed to get</u>?

D Which of these ideas does the article suggest? Check (✓) the boxes.

☐ All child actors have problems as they grow up.

☐ It is possible to be both a successful child and adult actor.

☐ Portman's career went downhill for a while.

☐ If Portman's parents hadn't made her study, she would have failed school.

☐ Radcliffe and Watson were both good students.

☐ As adults, all these former child actors are still successful.

☐ These actors became successful only due to the support of their parents.

2 Speaking and listening Success is . . .

A **Pair work** How do you define success? Discuss the ideas below and add your own.

being famous	having an important job	finding the right partner
enjoying life every day	doing fulfilling work	having lots of money

"I think you're successful if you become famous."

B ◀)) 4.08 Listen to four people talk about success. What does success mean to them? Complete the sentences with ideas from above.

1. For Isabel, success is _____.

2. For Claire, success is _____.

3. For Carlo, success is _____.

4. For Vivian, success is _____.

C ◀)) 4.08 Listen again. Do they think they have achieved success? Complete the chart.

	Are they successful?	Why do they think they are or aren't successful?
1. Isabel	Yes / No	_____
2. Claire	Yes / No	_____
3. Carlo	Yes / No	_____
4. Vivian	Yes / No	_____

3 Writing A success story

A Think of someone you know who has achieved success in some way. Make a list of reasons why he or she became successful. Then write a paragraph about him or her.

My successful friend

My friend Alexis is already a successful doctor at the age of 30, even though she had a difficult childhood in many ways. Her parents divorced when she was three, and she spent her early years moving from town to town and school to school. . . .

Help note

Topic and supporting sentences

Topic sentences state an idea or a theme.

Supporting sentences add more information or give examples.

B Read your classmates' paragraphs. Are any of the stories inspiring?

Free talk p. 133

Vocabulary notebook / Do your best!

Learning tip *Learning idioms*

Idioms are expressions in which the meaning isn't obvious from the individual words. When you learn a new idiom, it helps to write an example sentence that explains or clarifies its meaning.

In conversation

Fame and fortune
The words most likely to be used with *fame* are:
1. fame *and fortune*
2. *gained* fame
3. *hall of* fame
4. *claim to* fame
5. *achieved* fame

1 Match these sentences containing idioms with the explanations on the right.

1. He's been <u>in the headlines</u> a lot lately. _c_
2. He's <u>getting</u> a lot of <u>bad press</u>. ____
3. He's an <u>up-and-coming</u> actor. ____
4. His <u>career</u> has really <u>taken off</u>. ____
5. He <u>got discovered</u> very young. ____
6. He <u>had connections</u> in the industry. ____
7. He's really <u>dropped out of sight</u>. ____
8. His acting <u>career</u> is <u>going downhill</u>. ____

a. His career is going really well.
b. People think he's going to be a great actor.
c. He's been in the news.
d. You don't hear about him anymore.
e. He knew people who helped his career.
f. He's getting fewer and fewer acting roles.
g. He started his career at a young age.
h. The news media are criticizing him.

2 Word builder Now write explanation sentences for these idioms. Find out the meaning of any expressions you don't know.

1. A lot of young people really <u>look up to</u> pop stars. _____
2. My friend is a great singer. She's going to <u>go a long way</u>. _____
3. Some rock bands are still <u>going strong</u> after 20 or 30 years. _____
4. That young actor is going to <u>make a name for himself</u>. _____
5. She <u>knew the right people</u>, so she got the part. _____
6. He came to the city to try to <u>get into show business</u>. _____

Basketball Heroes

 On your own

Make a list of 10 famous people you like. Can you use a different idiomatic expression about each person?

I really look up to him.

1. Sun Ming Ming

✓ Can Do! Now I can . . .

✓ I can . . .   ? I need to review how to . . .

- [ ] talk hypothetically about the past.
- [ ] talk about celebrities and being famous.
- [ ] use tag questions to give opinions and check information.
- [ ] use tag questions to soften advice.

- [ ] answer difficult questions with expressions like *It's hard to say.*
- [ ] understand someone giving advice.
- [ ] understand people talking about success.
- [ ] read an article about child stars.
- [ ] write a profile of a successful person.

Trends

✓ Can Do! **In this unit, you learn how to . . .**

Lesson A
- Talk about social changes using the passive of the present continuous and present perfect

Lesson B
- Discuss the environment
- Use expressions like *although*, *because of*, *in order to*, and *instead*

Lesson C
- Use expressions like *As I said* to refer back in a conversation
- Use vague expressions like *and so forth*

Lesson D
- Read an article about success via the Internet
- Write a post for a website about technological trends

1

2

3

4

Before you begin . . .

Do any of these issues affect your city or country? Is the situation changing? What is the trend?

- traffic congestion
- work / life balance
- pollution
- an aging population
- urban development
- high unemployment

What social changes have you noticed recently?

1 "A lot of people are obsessed with losing weight and eating healthy foods. So the fast-food chains have been forced to change their menus. Now you can get salads and healthy stuff there as well as burgers and fries. And that's a good thing because obesity has become a big problem."

– Jake,
New York City

2 "Well, people are talking about losing their jobs. In many places, unemployment is going up, and a lot of people have been laid off. And that's partly because their jobs are being outsourced to workers in other countries."

– Letitia,
Detroit

3 "I think, like everywhere else, the main thing is the spread of technology. I mean, almost everyone I know has a cell phone now . . . and wireless Internet access is being made available in more and more places."

– Daniela,
Monterrey

4 "We have a lot of problems with traffic congestion. Fortunately, a lot of new highways have been built, and there's a new monorail, but the problem hasn't been completely solved. So, commuting can still be a real problem."

– Somchai,
Bangkok

5 "Well, young people are still being encouraged to go to college, which is good. It can be tough, though, because tuition fees have just been increased, and we're not being given enough financial support."

– Oliver,
Manchester, UK

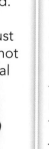

6 "Well, with the economic boom in recent years, one thing here is the shortage of skilled labor. There's a big demand for that now, so skilled workers are being recruited overseas, and then they're being brought in to fill the jobs."

– Ivan,
Moscow

1 Getting started

A Have any of these issues been in the news recently? Why? Tell the class.

_____ college tuition fees	_____ obesity	_____ shortage of skilled workers
_____ new technology	_____ outsourcing jobs	_____ traffic congestion

B 🔊)) 4.09 **Listen. Which of the issues above are the people talking about? Number the issues 1 to 6.**

Figure it out **C** How do the people express the ideas below? Rewrite the sentences.

1. They are encouraging young people to go to college.

2. They are not giving us enough financial support.

3. People have forced fast-food chains to change their menus.

4. They haven't completely solved the problem.

2 Grammar The passive ◀)) 4.10

Extra practice p. 150

> **The passive of present continuous and present perfect**
>
> | **Use the active form of a verb to focus on the "doer" or cause of the action.** | **Use the passive form to focus on the "receiver" of the action.** |
> |---|---|
> | Companies **are recruiting** workers overseas. They **are making** Internet access available. | Workers **are being recruited** overseas. Internet access **is being made** available. |
> | Companies **have laid off** a lot of people. They **haven't solved** the traffic problem. | A lot of people **have been laid off**. The traffic problem **hasn't been solved**. |

A Rewrite the comments, using the passive forms of the underlined verbs. Then compare with a partner.

That problem hasn't been solved yet. . . .

1. Teen car accidents are still a big concern for parents. They haven't solved that problem yet. However, they are advertising tracking devices. They've developed these devices to track speed. Some even turn the radio down. Apparently, they have saved a lot of lives.

2. They're providing healthier lunches in high schools now. They haven't taken junk food off menus completely. But they're not using processed food – well, not as much. Also, they're serving more organic foods.

3. They're developing the city center. They've knocked down a lot of older buildings, and they've built a lot of new hotels and offices. They're not solving the housing shortage, though. They're building too few homes.

About you **B** Group work Discuss the different trends in this lesson. Which are good? Which are not? Which are happening where you live? What other trends are there?

"Some roads in the city center are being closed to traffic. It's great. There are more outdoor cafés . . . "

3 Speaking naturally Reducing auxiliary verbs

> | | |
> |---|---|
> | *The education system **is** being reformed.* | (system**'s** being) |
> | *The education system **has** been reformed.* | (system**'s** been) |
> | *A lot of new schools **are** being built.* | (schools**'re** being) |
> | *A lot of new schools **have** been built.* | (schools**'ve** been) |

A ◀)) 4.11 Listen and repeat the sentences above. Notice the reduction of the auxiliary verbs.

About you **B** ◀)) 4.12 Listen and complete the sentences. Are they true in your country? Are they good ideas? Discuss your views with a partner.

1. More women _____ encouraged to train as science and engineering teachers.

2. Bilingual programs _____ offered to elementary school students.

3. Students _____ required to do community service.

4. Education _____ given more funding.

5. Technology _____ introduced into more classrooms.

6. Courses _____ made available for more people in the community.

Building vocabulary and grammar

A Complete the article with words and expressions from the box. What do you learn?

air pollution	drought	environmentally friendly	a landfill	toxic chemicals
biodegradable	energy-saving	global warming	✓natural resources	water consumption

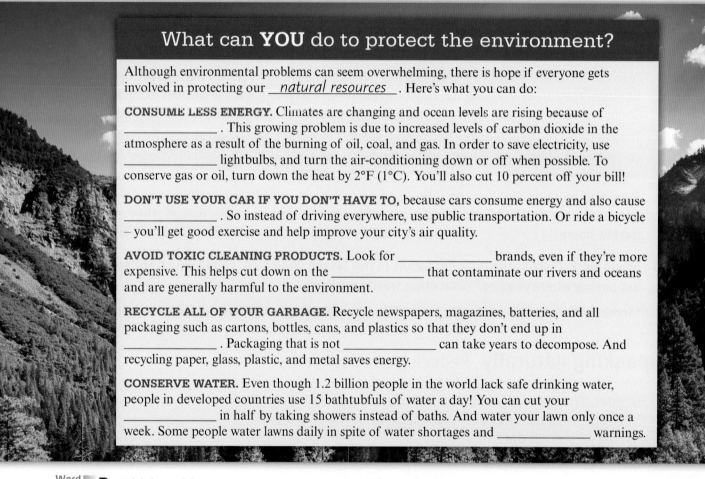

What can **YOU** do to protect the environment?

Although environmental problems can seem overwhelming, there is hope if everyone gets involved in protecting our ___natural resources___ . Here's what you can do:

CONSUME LESS ENERGY. Climates are changing and ocean levels are rising because of _____ . This growing problem is due to increased levels of carbon dioxide in the atmosphere as a result of the burning of oil, coal, and gas. In order to save electricity, use _____ lightbulbs, and turn the air-conditioning down or off when possible. To conserve gas or oil, turn down the heat by 2°F (1°C). You'll also cut 10 percent off your bill!

DON'T USE YOUR CAR IF YOU DON'T HAVE TO, because cars consume energy and also cause _____ . So instead of driving everywhere, use public transportation. Or ride a bicycle – you'll get good exercise and help improve your city's air quality.

AVOID TOXIC CLEANING PRODUCTS. Look for _____ brands, even if they're more expensive. This helps cut down on the _____ that contaminate our rivers and oceans and are generally harmful to the environment.

RECYCLE ALL OF YOUR GARBAGE. Recycle newspapers, magazines, batteries, and all packaging such as cartons, bottles, cans, and plastics so that they don't end up in _____ . Packaging that is not _____ can take years to decompose. And recycling paper, glass, plastic, and metal saves energy.

CONSERVE WATER. Even though 1.2 billion people in the world lack safe drinking water, people in developed countries use 15 bathtubfuls of water a day! You can cut your _____ in half by taking showers instead of baths. And water your lawn only once a week. Some people water lawns daily in spite of water shortages and _____ warnings.

Word sort **B** Which problems are you concerned about (or not)? What do you do, or not do? Make a chart like this with ideas from the article, and add your own. Compare with a partner.

I'm concerned about . . .	I'm not concerned about . . .
global warming. I don't use my car for short trips.	conserving water. I take baths. I don't take showers.

Figure it out **C** Can you choose the correct expression to complete each sentence? Compare with a partner. Are the sentences true for you?

Vocabulary notebook p. 116

1. I buy rechargeable batteries **in spite of / even though** the extra cost.

2. **Because / Because of** cars cause air pollution, I always take public transportation.

3. I turn down the air conditioning **in order to / so that** use less electricity.

4. I recycle cans **instead of / so** throwing them in the trash.

2 Grammar Linking ideas 🔊 4.13

Extra practice p. 150

Contrast	**Although / Even though** environmental problems are overwhelming, there is hope. Some people water their lawns daily **in spite of / despite** drought warnings.
Reason	Climates are changing **because of / as a result of / due to** global warming. Carbon dioxide levels are increasing **because** we are burning oil, coal, and gas.
Purpose	Turn down the air-conditioning **(in order) to** save electricity. Recycle garbage **so (that)** it doesn't end up in a landfill.
Alternative	Use public transportation **instead of** driving your car. Take showers **instead of** baths.

Notice:
in order to / *to* + **verb**
although / *even though* / *because* / *so that* / *so* + **clause**
in spite of / *despite* / *because of* / *as a result of* / *due to* / *instead of* + **noun (or verb + *-ing*)**

A Link the ideas in these sentences using expressions from the grammar chart. How many ways can you complete each sentence? Compare with a partner.

> ❌ **Common errors**
>
> Don't write *even though* or *in spite of* as one word.
>
> **Even though** *fuel is expensive, I drive my car a lot.*
> (NOT ~~Eventhough~~ *fuel is expensive, I drive my car a lot.*)

1. <u>*Even though / Although*</u> there are a lot of environmental problems, the situation isn't hopeless.

2. It's better to use everyday items to clean your home _____ buying expensive cleaning products. For example, you can use vinegar to clean your mirrors _____ toxic chemicals.

3. _____ cut down on the paper you use, get all your bills delivered online.

4. A lot of vegetables from local areas are being sold in stores _____ consumer pressure. This is good _____ it supports local farmers and cuts down on transportation.

5. A lot of areas are being affected by air pollution _____ efforts to improve air quality. Ride a bicycle or walk _____ using the car. Or, if you buy a new car, get a hybrid vehicle _____ you can save on gas.

6. If you buy bottled water, make sure the bottle is biodegradable _____ you can prevent buildup in landfills.

7. There is more solar and wind power now _____ advances in technology. However, _____ recent advances, they're not being used as widely as they could be by consumers.

8. _____ we need to preserve our natural resources, we also need to use oil and gas for energy.

About you **B** Pair work Discuss the ideas above. Which ones do you agree with?

3 Talk about it Saving the planet

Group work Discuss the environmental problems below. What other problems are there? Which are the most serious? What is being done to solve the problems? What else could be done?

- ▸ air and water pollution
- ▸ global warming
- ▸ depletion of oil reserves
- ▸ nuclear waste disposal
- ▸ garbage in landfills
- ▸ endangered species

A *Even though air pollution is getting worse, not much is being done about it.*

B *Well, "no-drive" days are being introduced in order to cut down on traffic on the worst days.*

🔊 **Sounds right** p. 139

1 Conversation strategy   Referring back in the conversation

A Read the comment below. What other workplace trends are making companies family-friendly?

Adam *"I think there's a trend toward companies becoming family-friendly. For example, a lot of men are being offered paid leave when they become fathers."*

B 🔊 4.14 Listen. What other changes in the workplace do Adam, Celia, and Greg talk about?

Adam	As I was saying, companies are definitely more family-friendly these days. And like I said, there's more paternity leave, flexible hours, child-care centers, and so on.
Celia	Yeah. There are definitely more benefits and incentives for working parents. I think companies need to attract and keep good employees.
Greg	Right. And going back to what you were saying about benefits, a lot more people are being encouraged to telecommute instead of working at the office.
Celia	I think companies do it in order to save on costs. And with things like email, and web conferencing, and so forth, it's no problem.
Greg	I'm sure they get increased productivity, too. Fewer interruptions, fewer meetings, etc.
Adam	You mentioned earlier, Celia, about saving on costs. There seems to be a trend, too, toward offering internships to young people.
Celia	Right. I mean, it's a great way to get experience and contacts, and so forth . . .
Greg	Yeah, but basically it's just unpaid work.

C Notice how Adam, Celia, and Greg use expressions like these to refer back to things said earlier. Find examples.

You / I mentioned . . . earlier.	
As / Like	I said / I was saying . . .
Going back to what	you said / you were saying . . .

D 🔊 4.15 Listen to more of the conversation. Write the expressions you hear. Then discuss the ideas with a partner. Do you agree with any of them?

Greg I mean, _____, Celia, companies want to save on costs.

Celia But _____, it's good experience. And internships can lead to full-time jobs.

Adam True. And companies can see if someone is a good fit before they hire them. _____, Celia, they need good employees. It's _____, people want good benefits.

Celia Right. And _____, Greg, telecommuting is a kind of benefit.

2 Strategy plus *and so forth*

In more formal settings, use vague expressions like ***and so forth***, ***and so on***, and ***etc.***, instead of informal expressions like ***and things like that***.

etc. = et cetera

And like I said, there's more paternity leave, flexible hours, child-care centers, and so on.

In conversation

Informal vague expressions like ***and things like that*** are more common than formal ones.

▬▬▬▬▬ *and things like that*
▬▬▬ *and so forth*
▬ *and so on*
▪ *etc.*

About you ■ **Complete the sentences with the words in the box, and add a vague expression. Then discuss with a partner. Do you agree?**

| equal pay | health insurance | improve their résumés | less time off | restaurants |

1. Due to the state of the economy, people are being forced to work harder, with longer hours, _____ .

2. Companies should offer more benefits, like more vacation days, better _____ .

3. Men and women should be treated equally, with equal chances of promotion and _____ .

4. Young people do internships because of the opportunity they get to gain experience, _____ .

5. In order to survive, people are being forced to work into their 70s and 80s, in stores and _____ .

"People are being forced to work harder. Most people I know work late and work on the weekends, and so on."

3 Listening and strategies Trends in the workplace

A Look at the sentences below. Can you guess what else the people might say?

☐ As I was saying, working from home has some disadvantages, for example . . .

☐ Going back to what you were saying about desk sharing, it's good because . . .

☐ Going back to what you said about working flexible hours, it makes sense because . . .

☐ I mentioned earlier that calls and email are being monitored more. It's necessary . . .

☐ As I said, paternity leave isn't being offered in some companies, but . . .

B ◀)) 4.16 Listen to extracts from four conversations. Which of the topics above are the people discussing? Number the sentences 1 to 4. There is one extra sentence.

C ◀)) 4.16 Listen again. Write one advantage and one disadvantage of each trend.

About you ■ **D Pair work Discuss each trend. What other advantages are there? What are other disadvantages? Which benefit would you most like to have?**

Free talk p. 135

1 Reading

A How do people use the Internet to promote themselves? List as many ways as possible.

"They post videos of their singing or acting."
"They create websites on a specific topic. They write interesting blogs."

> **Reading tip**
>
> As you read, ask yourself questions like, "Is this true?" "So, what does this mean?" "What examples can I think of?"

B Read the article. What are the three people mentioned in the article famous for?

---

http://www.internetsuccesses... 🔍

The Internet — The new pathway to success?

Years ago, the path to success in the world of entertainment seemed long and arduous. Aspiring artists often waited years before being noticed by the public. There were endless stories of actors waiting tables in Hollywood hoping to get discovered; of writers sending off hundreds of manuscripts to publishers only to accumulate a pile of rejection letters; of singers working for next to nothing in small clubs as they waited to get signed by a record company. Nowadays, however, instead of depending on big media companies to decide their future, more and more artists are following the trend of displaying their talents online – often with spectacular results.

Pop star Justin Bieber is perhaps the best-known Internet success story. This self-taught musician was a fifteen-year-old Canadian high school student whose only claim to fame was a second-place prize in a local talent show. When his mother began posting videos of Justin singing on the Internet, he became an "overnight sensation." Within months he was signing a contract with a major record label, and his first full-length album, *My World 2.0*, hit the charts around the world.

A growing number of novelists are gaining recognition on the Internet, too. That's where Darcie Chan self-published her first novel as an e-book even though it was rejected by ten publishers and more than a hundred literary agents. The novel, *The Mill River Recluse*, sold 400,000 copies in its first year. As a result of that success, Chan is now being courted by major publishers and even by movie studios.

A different sort of fame has been achieved by Michelle Phan, who got her start with online video tutorials on beauty and cosmetics. Within a few years, she had over 200 videos to her credit, and more than one *billion* Internet views. She has now been hired by a major cosmetics company to promote their products online.

Clearly, because of the Internet, talented people are increasingly less dependent on the power of the publishing, music, and movie industries. Of course, most stories of Internet success are much more modest. When a video of a cat playing the piano or a child singing opera goes viral, the fame doesn't last very long. As the artist Andy Warhol famously predicted in 1968: "In the future, everyone will be world-famous for 15 minutes." It's a prediction that certainly appears to be coming true. Who knows who or what trend will emerge in the next 15 minutes? Your guess is as a good as mine.

C Rewrite the questions below, replacing the underlined words with similar expressions from the article. Then read the article again, and ask and answer the questions with a partner.

1. When Justin Bieber was in high school, what was his reason for being well known?
2. Who helped Justin Bieber become an instant success on the Internet? How did it happen?
3. How did the Internet help Darcie Chan become respected as an author? What were the results?
4. How many video tutorials does Michelle Phan have that she has made herself? What evidence is there of her success?
5. What are some examples of Internet videos that become extremely popular very quickly?

D **Pair work** Discuss the questions with a partner.

1. What are some things aspiring artists used to do in order to get noticed? Name three things.

2. Do you know of other people who followed the same route to success as Justin Bieber, Darcie Chan, or Michelle Phan?

3. In what way is Andy Warhol's famous prediction coming true? Can you think of examples?

4. How will things change for publishers, record labels, and movie studios in the future?

2 Listening and writing Trends in technology

A 🔊 **4.17** Listen to four people talk about recent trends. What trends are they talking about? Write *a* to *d*. Then decide if the person feels positive (P) or negative (N) about the trend. Circle *P* or *N*.

1. Adam _____ (P / N)
2. Emily _____ (P / N)
3. Tyler _____ (P / N)
4. Madison _____ (P / N)

   a. home media systems
   b. typing technology
   c. phone use in social situations
   d. online shopping

B 🔊 **4.17** Listen again. Why does each person like or dislike the new trend? Write at least one reason.

1. Adam: _____

2. Emily: _____

3. Tyler: _____

4. Madison: _____

About you **C** **Pair work** Think of a trend in technology that has affected you. How has it changed your life? Do you feel positive or negative about it? Write down some notes. Then discuss it with your partner.

D Read the comment on a technology website and the Help note. Underline the expressions the writer uses to describe a trend. Then use your notes from Exercise C to write a similar post.

posted 3 hours ago

The trend away from laptops

Recently I've noticed that my friends and I are spending less time on our laptops and more and more time on our smartphones. Phones used to be used mainly for texting and for taking and sending photos, while laptops were used for everything else, like answering email, watching videos, getting directions, or searching the Internet. As people increasingly use their smartphones for these functions, the use of laptops is declining. For me, at least, this is a good change. I used to carry a heavy laptop from café to café in order to access the Internet. Now I can go online without paying for an expensive cup of coffee!

David128

 Help note

Describing trends

*We're spending **more and more** time on our smartphones.*

*We're spending **less** time / **fewer** hours on our laptops.*

*People **increasingly** use their phones for a variety of functions.*

*The use of laptops is **decreasing** / **declining**.*

*The number of smartphones is **increasing** / **growing**.*

About you **E** **Group work** Read your group's posts. Have you all noticed the same trends? Discuss.

Vocabulary notebook / Try to explain it!

In conversation

It's in the air!
The type of pollution people talk about most is *air pollution*.

Learning tip *Writing definitions in your own words*

When you learn a new word or expression, you can write a definition or explanation in your own words to help you remember its meaning.

1 Match the expressions with their definitions or explanations.

1. The **atmosphere** refers to __e__
2. **Carbon dioxide** is a gas in the atmosphere _____
3. If you **consume** something, _____
4. **Air quality** refers to _____
5. When there is a **water shortage**, _____
6. If something is **toxic** to the environment, _____
7. When you **recycle** something, _____
8. If something **decomposes**, _____

a. you use it up, and it can't be used again.
b. there isn't enough water for people.
c. you use it again instead of throwing it away.
d. it contaminates or pollutes the environment.
e. the air around the Earth.
f. that is produced when things burn or decay.
g. it decays, or breaks down into simple elements.
h. how much pollution is in the air.

2 Write sentences that define or explain these words.

air pollution	drought	global warming	toxic chemicals
biodegradable	environmentally friendly	a landfill	water consumption

3 **Word builder** Find out the meaning of these words and expressions. Then write a sentence to define or explain each one.

deforestation	fossil fuels	hybrid cars	pesticides
extinction	the greenhouse effect	the ozone layer	renewable energy

On your own

Post notes around your home in English reminding you to turn off the lights, recycle bottles, and so on.

 Can Do! Now I can . . .

✓ I can . . .   ❓ I need to review how to . . .

- ☐ talk about social changes.
- ☐ talk about environmental problems.
- ☐ link ideas with expressions like *although*, *because of*, *in order to*, and *instead*.
- ☐ refer back to points made earlier in the conversation.

- ☐ use formal vague expressions.
- ☐ understand a discussion about workplace trends.
- ☐ understand conversations about technology trends.
- ☐ read an article about success via the Internet.
- ☐ write a comment for a website about technological trends

✓ **Can Do!** In this unit, you learn how to . . .

Lesson A
- Discuss career planning using *What* clauses and long noun phrases

Lesson B
- Discuss job prospects
- Talk about your career plans using the future continuous and future perfect

Lesson C
- Introduce what you say with expressions like *What I read was*
- Say *I don't know if . . .* to introduce ideas

Lesson D
- Read an article on how to answer tough interview questions
- Write a cover letter for a job application

Before you begin . . .

Which of these areas of work are hard to get into? Which are easier? Which are the highest paid? Which are the most popular with your friends?

- the media
- hotel and tourism
- medicine
- law
- finance
- entertainment
- social work
- teaching
- trades (carpentry, plumbing)

What's the best way to go about choosing a career?

Laura

I think the first thing to do is to decide on an area you're interested in. And then do some research to find out what jobs you can do in that area. I mean, what I'd do first is talk to people and find out what jobs they do. And maybe find out more on the Internet. The main thing you need is lots of information.

Jacob

Yeah, for sure. What you should do is think about what you really enjoy doing with your time. And then see if you can make a career out of it. The good thing about that is you end up with a job you love. I guess what I'm saying is that you need to choose a career you'll really like.

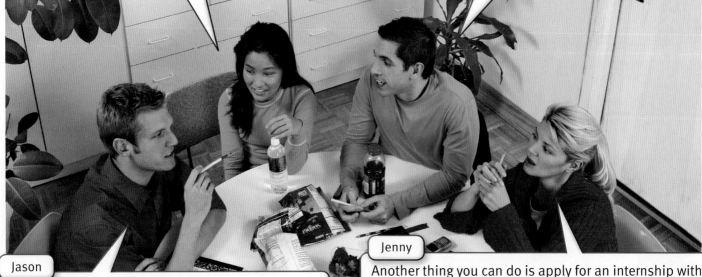

Jason

Right. And one thing I would do is see a career counselor and take one of those personality tests to find out what your strengths and weaknesses are. And then the career counselors . . . well, what they do is tell you what kinds of jobs you'd be good at.

Jenny

Another thing you can do is apply for an internship with a company. The advantage of that is that you get some work experience while you're still in school. What a friend of mine did was interesting. What she did was call up a bunch of companies and offer to work for free on her vacations. She got some great experience that way.

1 Getting started

A Which of these do you think are the best three ways to choose a career? Tell the class.

- ☐ do an internship
- ☐ talk to a career counselor
- ☐ do research online
- ☐ go to a job fair
- ☐ take a personality test
- ☐ ask a friend for advice

B ◀)) 4.18 Listen to four students talk about ways to choose a career. Which of the ideas above do they mention? Check (✓) the ideas. What other ideas do they suggest?

Figure it out **C** How do the people above say these things? Underline what they say in the discussion.

1. Jenny   A friend of mine did something interesting. She called up a bunch of companies.

2. Jacob   I guess I'm saying that you need to choose a career you'll really like.

3. Laura   First you need to decide on an area you're interested in.

4. Jason   I would see a career counselor.

Grammar *What* clauses; long noun phrase subjects ◀)) **4.19**

Extra practice p. 151

What clauses and long noun phrases introduce important information. They are often the subject of the verb *be*, which can be followed by a word or a phrase (noun, adjective, or verb) or by a clause.

What clauses	Long noun phrases
What you need is lots of information.	**The main thing you need** is information.
What my friend did was interesting.	**Something my friend did** was interesting.
What I would do is talk to people.	**The best thing to do** is (to) talk to people.
What I'm saying is (that) you need to choose a career you'll really like.	**The good thing about that** is (that) you end up with a job you love.

A Choose the best expression on the right to complete each sentence.
Once you've chosen a career, how do you go about getting your dream job?

1. Well, ____*the best thing to do*____ is to make contacts and network with people. _____ is ask all my friends and family if they know anyone who could help me. _____ is it could help you get an interview.

   the good thing about that
   ✓the best thing to do
   what I would do

2. _____ is get some work experience. _____ is it helps you find out if you'd really like a job in that area. _____ is try it out first.

   what I'm saying
   the advantage of that
   what I would do first

3. _____ was get an internship. She said _____ is a good reference letter. Then _____ was interesting. She just walked into several different companies and introduced herself.

   the main thing you need
   something my friend did
   what she did

4. _____ is a good résumé. _____ was good. She got hers done professionally. _____ is you make a really good first impression.

   the best thing about that
   what my classmate did
   what you need

About you **B** **Pair work** How would you go about getting your dream job? Discuss ideas.

A *What I'd do first is update my social networking site and say I'm looking for a job.*
B *That's a good idea. The best thing to do is tell all your contacts.*

3 **Speaking naturally** Stressing *I* and *you*

Anne *What would you do if you found your dream job and then hated it?*
Matt *I don't know. What would **you** do if **you** hated your dream job, Cate?*
Cate *I have no idea what I'd do.*
Enzo *I know what **I** would do. I'd quit immediately. Life's too short. How about **you**?*

A ◀)) **4.20** Listen and repeat the conversation. Notice how *I* and *you* are sometimes stressed to make clear who you are talking about. Then practice and continue the conversation with a partner.

B **Group work** Discuss the questions. Stress *I* and *you* if you need to.

- What's the best way to choose a career?
- What have some of your friends done to find work?
- What can you do if you can't decide on a career?

1 Building vocabulary and grammar

A **4.21** Listen and read the interviews. What career plans do these students have?

Where do you think you'll be working five years from now?

Well, I'll have finished my degree in media studies by then, and what I really want to do is get a job in **communications.** You won't be seeing me on TV or anything – I'm not cut out for that – but I may be working in, like, **publishing** or **journalism** as an **editor** or writer or something. Or maybe I'll have gotten a job in **advertising** or **public relations.** That would be fun.
– Ashley

Well, in two years, I'll be graduating with a degree in **nursing** – so I'll be working in the field of **health care.** One thing I think I'd like to do is be a **psychiatric nurse,** but I'm not sure. Hopefully my wife will have graduated from medical school by then, too. She'd like to be a **pediatrician** . . . or else a **surgeon.**
– Albert

I won't be doing what I'm doing now – **telemarketing** – that's for sure! This fall, I'll be starting a degree in **business management,** so in five years, I'll have graduated and gotten a job in the **construction industry.** I probably won't have had much experience, but I'll be working with **civil engineers, contractors, construction workers,** and so on. – Jesse

Hopefully I'll be working as a **financial analyst** in an investment bank. My dad's a **stockbroker,** and my mom's a **tax adviser,** so I guess I'm following them into the **financial sector.** – Simone

I don't really know. I just hope I'll be using my languages. I might be working as an **interpreter** or a **translator** – or maybe I'll be working in the **travel industry.** – Cheryl

Word sort **B** Make a word web for each area of work. Add more jobs. Then compare with a partner. Which jobs do you think would be interesting? fun? well paid? rewarding?

Construction industry	Medicine and health care
Financial services	Travel industry
Media and communications	Sales and marketing

civil engineer
Construction industry – architect

Figure it out **C** Can you make these sentences true by changing the underlined words? Compare with a partner.

Vocabulary notebook p. 126

1. Jesse will be working in telemarketing in five years.
2. In two years, Albert won't be graduating with a degree in nursing.
3. Cheryl will be working as a translator five years from now.
4. Five years from now, Ashley will be studying for her degree in media studies.

Grammar The future continuous and future perfect 🔊 **4.22**

Extra practice p. 151

Use the future continuous for ongoing activities in the future.
I'll be working in health care.
I won't be working in this job.

Also use it for events you expect to happen.
I'll be graduating in two years.
I'll be starting a degree this fall.

You can use *might* and *may* instead of *will*.
I may be working in publishing.

Use the future perfect for events that are in the past when you "view" them from the future.
My wife **will have graduated** by then.
I probably **won't have had** much experience.

> **In conversation**
> The future continuous is much more common than the future perfect.

A Complete the conversations using the future continuous or future perfect. Then practice with a partner.

1. A What do you think you'll _____ (do) five years from now?
   B I hope I'll _____ (work) as an architect. I'll _____ (finish) all the exams by then. How about you?
   A Well, by then I'll _____ (graduate), too – I hope to finish my nursing degree in two years. I might _____ (work) in a medical practice.

2. A Do you have any idea what your life will be like in ten years?
   B Well, I hope I'll _____ (enjoy) life. I think my boyfriend and I will _____ (get) married by then, and maybe we'll _____ (buy) our own home. I'm not sure if we'll _____ (start) a family, but if we have kids, I think I'll _____ (take) care of them, and I may _____ (work) part-time, too.

3. A What do you think you'll _____ (do) when you're 60?
   B Well, I probably won't _____ (stop) working, but I hope I won't _____ (work) long hours every day.
   A Me too. Maybe by then I'll _____ (retired), and I'll _____ (live) by the ocean.

4. A What kinds of jobs do you think people will _____ (do) 20 years from now?
   B I think more people will _____ (work) in health care because people will _____ (live) longer. Also the retirement age will _____ (rise), too, so people might still _____ (work) when they're 70.

About you **B** **Pair work** Ask and answer the questions. Give your own answers. Do you have similar hopes and dreams?

> **✗ Common errors**
> When you are making arrangements, use the future continuous to announce your intentions.
> *See you at 6.* ***I'll be waiting*** *for you in the lobby.* OR *I'll wait . . .* (NOT ~~I'm waiting~~ . . .)

 Talk about it Working lives

Group work Discuss the statements. Do you agree with them?

Ten years from now, . . .
- more people will be working from home.
- fewer people will have had a college education.
- people will be retiring at a younger age.
- people will still be learning English to help them with their careers.
- the working day will have become shorter.

Sounds right p. 139

The best part was . . .

1 Conversation strategy Introducing what you say

A What kinds of summer jobs do students do? Make a list.

B 🔊 4.23 Listen to Jin-ho and Jenn. What does Jenn say about working at the theme park?

Jin-ho	Didn't you work in that theme park last summer?
Jenn	Yeah. In the ticket booth for the concert arena.
Jin-ho	Really? How was it? The reason I ask is I was wondering about applying for a job there myself.
Jenn	It was good. I mean, the best part was that I got to go on all the rides for free. I don't know if you know, but you get a free season pass.
Jin-ho	Cool.
Jenn	Yeah. And what I thought was really good was I got to see a lot of the concerts and meet some of the performers backstage.
Jin-ho	Great. Now, what I heard was that it's hard to get a job there.
Jenn	Well, yeah. What I was going to tell you was that they have a job fair in the spring. I don't know if you're familiar with one, but you go around the park and interview for different jobs.
Jin-ho	Yeah? Maybe I should go to that.

C Notice how Jin-ho and Jenn introduce what they say with expressions like these. Find the expressions they use.

> *What I thought was good was (that) . . .*
> *The best part is / was (that) . . .*
> *What I heard / read was (that) . . .*
> *The reason I ask is (that) . . .*
> *What I was going to tell you / say was (that) . . .*

D 🔊 4.24 Listen. Write the expressions Jin-ho and Jenn use. Then practice.

1. **Jenn** Have you had any experience? _____ it helps when you have previous work experience.

   Jin-ho Actually, yeah. I worked in a restaurant one time. _____ I got good tips.

2. **Jin-ho** So what will you be doing during summer break?

   Jenn I'll be working as a camp counselor this year. My friend did it last year. She said it was great. _____ she got to go rafting and everything with the kids *and* she got paid for it.

3. **Jin-ho** How old were you when you got your first job? _____ my sister wants to work, but she's only 15.

   Jenn _____ you have to be 16 before you can get a job. But I'm not sure.

About you **E** **Pair work** Discuss the questions above. Give your own answers. Introduce what you say with expressions from the box.

2 Strategy plus *I don't know if...*

> **I don't know if...**
> can introduce a statement, often
> to involve the other person in the topic.

> I don't know if you know, but
> you get a free season pass.

In conversation

Some of the most common expressions
with *I don't know if* are:

I don't know if you've (ever) heard...
I don't know if you're familiar with...
I don't know if you've (ever) seen...

A Rewrite the sentences. Use *I don't know if* to introduce the topics.

1. Have you ever worked in a restaurant? It's really hard work.

   *I don't know if you've ever worked in a restaurant,
   but it's really hard work.*

2. Have you ever sent out your résumé? Often companies don't bother to reply.

3. Have you read about this? One of the most popular careers is engineering.

4. Do you know? The main thing employers want is reliable workers.

5. Have you heard? More and more people work while they're on vacation.

6. Are you familiar with all those jobs websites? You can post your résumé on them.

7. Did you read? 80% of people are not satisfied with their jobs.

8. Have you heard this? On average, people in the U.S. change jobs seven times before they turn 30.

B **Pair work** Take turns saying the sentences to start conversations.

3 Listening and strategies An interesting job

A 🔊 4.25 Can you answer any of the questions below? Then listen to a personal trainer talk about her work. Which questions does she answer? Check (✓) the questions.

- ☐ What is a personal trainer's main role?
- ☐ Why do people hire personal trainers?
- ☐ How do you become a personal trainer?
- ☐ Is a personal trainer's job rewarding? Why?

- ☐ Are all trainers certified?
- ☐ What are the disadvantages of the job?
- ☐ How much do personal trainers earn?
- ☐ How do you find a good trainer?

B 🔊 4.25 Listen again. How does the personal trainer answer the questions? Write two pieces of information for each question.

About you **C** **Group work** Discuss the questions.

- What's the most unusual or interesting job you've heard about?
- What jobs do people you know have? Which is the most challenging? Why?
- Are there any jobs that you really wouldn't want to do? Why not?
- What's the first job you ever did? Was it fun?
- What would be an exciting job? Why?

   *"Well, I don't know if you've ever seen the work of an interior designer, but they seem to
   have a really interesting job. What I heard was..."*

1 Reading

A What would you do to prepare for a job interview? Make a class list.

"One thing you need to do is research the company."

B Look at the three interview questions in the article. How would you answer them? Compare your ideas with a partner. Then read the article. How would you change your answers?

> **Reading tip**
> Try to predict the "great answers" to the questions before you read them.

---

http://www.jobhunting... +

Ace that Interview! Tough Questions, Great Answers

Nothing can trip you up during an interview like an unexpected or difficult question. Whether you're applying for an internship, trying to get into college, or interviewing for a new job, here are a few questions that might stump you – along with the kinds of answers interviewers like to hear.

"Tell me about yourself."
Be ready to describe what makes you special as an individual. "What I *don't* want to hear is your life history," explains Dennis B., Director of Admissions at a major university. "I don't care how many siblings you have or where you were born. I want to know what makes you special. I want to see how well you project yourself, if you're articulate, and to hear your reasons for applying to do this course of study." The same applies at a job interview. Be concise and give concrete examples: "The main thing you should know about me is that while I was in college, I had a side job retrieving lost data from computers. I set up and marketed the business myself. I had 80 customers in the first year."

"What draws you to this line of work?"
Know what you're getting yourself into. "Publishing is a tough profession," says Tracy P., Editorial Director at a publishing house in New York City. "Unfortunately, some people want to get into it for the wrong reasons. Many candidates mention how much they love books and reading. However, that doesn't necessarily mean that editing or the business side of publishing is a good profession for you. You might be better suited to

teaching, for example. If someone doesn't understand the profession, the chances are they won't be a good fit for this type of work." In other words, show that you understand what the job involves in your response to the question and give an example of how you have acquired the relevant skills: "One skill you need to work in publishing is attention to detail. I worked on the college magazine and edited articles . . . "

"Tell me about a time you made a serious mistake. How did you handle it?"
"Many of our candidates get hired right after they graduate from college, before they've had a chance to get much work experience," notes Anita M., head of recruiting at a Fortune 500 financial company. "The reason I ask this question is that it's a tough question for everybody, and how a person answers is very revealing. It's important that people admit when they've made a mistake, rather than blame others. What I'm saying is that I expect candidates to be honest, and I look for signs that they've learned from the mistake." So, don't say you have never really made a mistake. Instead, try something along these lines: "One thing I did while I was working on a project in college was let down my team. I didn't complete my part of the project on time. I apologized. I also explained to the professor it was my fault and asked for an extension. Then I made it up to my teammates by working all weekend to finish the project. It taught me how to manage my time and not leave things until the last minute."

▶ **Remember:** Speak clearly and at a normal pace of conversation. Don't rush your words because you're nervous. Be calm and speak with confidence.

C **Pair work** Discuss your answers to the questions below.

1. What trips up some candidates during an interview, according to the article?
2. What mistake do some candidates make when they are asked to talk about themselves?
3. What two things do you need to tell an interviewer to show you're right for the job?
4. Why is it revealing when candidates talk about mistakes they have made?
5. Which question do you think is the most difficult one to answer? Why?

2 Listening and writing A fabulous opportunity!

A 🔊 4.26 Read the online job advertisement. Can you guess the missing words? Then listen to Maria talk about the ad with her friend Alex. Were any of your guesses correct?

Job summary

Company

——————

Location
Montreal

Job type
- Part-time
- ○ Full-time

Tour Guide

A leading tour company is seeking someone who would enjoy meeting ——————— from other countries. You must be fluent in ——————— and ——————— . You should be interested in the local area and its ——————— . You'll be traveling around the region ——————— days a week. Flexible, fun, and ——————— applicants only.

Apply by email, and also send your ——————— . Successful applicants will receive excellent pay and a generous benefits package.

APPLY

B 🔊 4.26 Listen again. Why is Maria perfect for this job? Write four reasons.

C Imagine you want to apply for the job above. Read the Help note and write a cover letter like the one below.

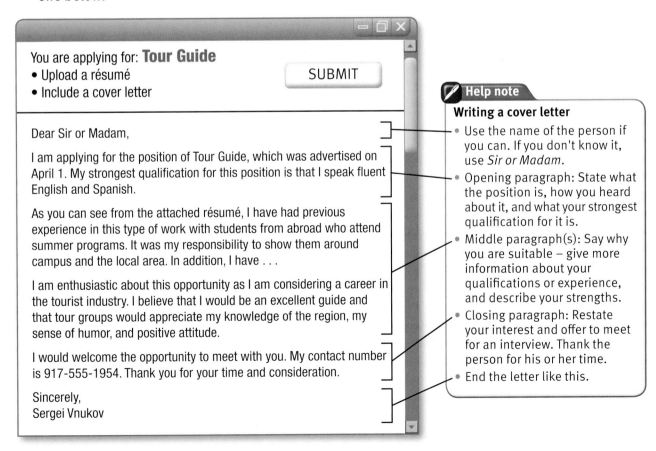

You are applying for: **Tour Guide**
- Upload a résumé
- Include a cover letter

SUBMIT

Dear Sir or Madam,

I am applying for the position of Tour Guide, which was advertised on April 1. My strongest qualification for this position is that I speak fluent English and Spanish.

As you can see from the attached résumé, I have had previous experience in this type of work with students from abroad who attend summer programs. It was my responsibility to show them around campus and the local area. In addition, I have . . .

I am enthusiastic about this opportunity as I am considering a career in the tourist industry. I believe that I would be an excellent guide and that tour groups would appreciate my knowledge of the region, my sense of humor, and positive attitude.

I would welcome the opportunity to meet with you. My contact number is 917-555-1954. Thank you for your time and consideration.

Sincerely,
Sergei Vnukov

Help note

Writing a cover letter
- Use the name of the person if you can. If you don't know it, use *Sir or Madam*.
- Opening paragraph: State what the position is, how you heard about it, and what your strongest qualification for it is.
- Middle paragraph(s): Say why you are suitable – give more information about your qualifications or experience, and describe your strengths.
- Closing paragraph: Restate your interest and offer to meet for an interview. Thank the person for his or her time.
- End the letter like this.

D **Group work** Read your classmates' cover letters. Who do you think should get the job?

Free talk p. 136

125

In conversation

Teachers are tops!
The job people talk about most is *teacher*.

Learning tip *Word building with roots and collocations*

When you learn a new word, you can expand your vocabulary quickly by learning

• other words with the same root.   • some common collocations.

journalism   journalist   *political journalist   freelance journalist*

1 Complete the chart with the areas of work and the jobs.

Area of work	Job		Area of work	Job		Area of work	Job
accounting	accountant			interpreter		psychiatry	
architecture			law				psychologist
	carpenter			manager			publisher
counseling				nurse		sales	
	dentist		pediatrics				surgeon
design				photographer		telemarketing	
editing			physical therapy				translator
	engineer			plumber			zoologist
financial analysis							

2 **Word builder** Match the words in **A** with the words in **B** to make common collocations. How many jobs can you make? Can you add any more words to make different job combinations?

A			B	
civil	psychiatric		analyst	technician
construction	social		engineer	worker
laboratory	systems		nurse	
pediatric				

On your own

Find a jobs website. Write the names of 20 different jobs in English.

✔ Can Do! Now I can . . .

✔ I can . . .   ? I need to review how to . . .

- [ ] talk about career planning.
- [ ] highlight important information.
- [ ] talk about professions and job prospects.
- [ ] talk about my future career plans.
- [ ] use expressions to introduce what I say.

- [ ] say *I don't know if* . . . to involve others.
- [ ] understand a conversation with a personal trainer.
- [ ] understand a discussion about a job advertisement.
- [ ] read an article about preparing for a job interview.
- [ ] write a cover letter for a job application.

1 Talking about jobs

Match the two parts of each sentence. Then discuss them with a partner. Add ideas and expressions like *and so on*, *and so forth*, and *etc*.

1. Being a surgeon is very rewarding, __*c*__
2. Stockbrokers are under a lot of stress _____
3. It's easy to get health-care jobs these days _____
4. Workers are being brought into the country _____
5. Plan your career in five-year blocks _____
6. More students are taking media studies, _____
7. There are fewer telemarketing jobs _____

a. even though really good jobs are hard to get.
b. in order to fill all the jobs in construction.
c. in spite of the long hours you have to work.
d. so that you can set realistic goals.
e. because of the shortage of nurses.
f. as a result of outsourcing to other countries.
g. due to the constant changes in financial markets.

"I imagine being a surgeon is rewarding, in spite of the long hours and the stress and so on."

2 How many words can you think of?

A Add six words and expressions to each category, and compare with a partner.

Being famous	The environment
in the headlines	

B Pair work Choose four items from each category to use in a conversation. How many different expressions can you remember to introduce what you say?

A I don't know if you've heard, but Angelina Jolie is in the headlines right now.
B Oh, yeah. What I heard was she recently . . .

3 What will life be like in 2030?

A Complete the sentences using the future continuous or future perfect.

1. Hopefully, by 2030, people __*will be buying*__ (buy) more and more environmentally friendly products, and we _____ (find) new ways to save energy, so we _____ (live) in a cleaner environment.

2. Ideally, we _____ (slow) global warming by then. We _____ (not use) fuels like coal anymore. More countries _____ (start) to use cleaner, more efficient fuels.

3. By 2030, people _____ (eat) healthier food, and the number of obese people _____ (decrease).

4. Because we _____ (live) longer, the percentage of older people in society _____ (rise) by then.

B Group work Discuss the sentences. Refer back to what people say with expressions like *As you said*, *Like you were saying*, and *Going back to . . .*. Add your opinions.

4 What if . . . ?

"I applied for an internship at a public relations company after college. At the end of my interview, they offered me a job. Now, 20 years later, I'm still there, and I'm vice president."

– Alice

"I was bored with my job at the bank, so I saw a career counselor and took some personality tests. They showed I was creative! So I went into advertising, and I love it."

– Martin

"I was going to major in math at college, but I got sick the first week and had to drop out. In the hospital, I got interested in nursing, and so now, here I am – a pediatric nurse."

– Alfonso

A Read the comments above. How might these people's lives have been different? Write sentences using *if* + the past perfect form and *would have, could have,* or *may / might have.*

If Alice hadn't applied for an internship at that company, she wouldn't have ended up working there.

B **Pair work** Talk about three big decisions you've made in life. Ask and answer hypothetical questions. If a question is difficult to answer, use an expression like *Good question.*

5 Check it out.

What do you know about your partner? Complete the sentences, adding tag questions. Then ask your partner.

1. You live in _____, ___*don't you*___ ?
2. You've studied English for _____ years, _____ ?
3. You don't like _____ music, _____ ?
4. You're a _____ , _____ ?
5. You went to _____ on vacation once, _____ ?

6 Any suggestions?

Complete the sentences using the passive of the present continuous or present perfect. Then role-play with a partner. Take turns making suggestions.

1. "We _'re being given_ (give) too much homework these days."
2. "I _____ (ask) to do volunteer work, but I'm too busy."
3. "I _____ (promote) at work, but I prefer my old job!"
4. "People _____ (lay off) at work recently. I'm worried because I _____ (pay) more than my co-workers."

A ***We're being given too much homework these days.***
B ***You could talk to your teacher about it, couldn't you?***

128

UNIT 7 Who gets help with something?

Class activity Ask and answer the questions. Find someone who answers yes. Ask questions to find out more information.

Do you know anyone who . . .

- gets family photos taken professionally?
- got someone to run an errand for them recently?
- has something at home that needs to be fixed?
- is having their house decorated?
- often gets a friend to help with homework?
- likes to get pizza delivered at home?
- got a tech center to solve a computer problem recently?
- owns something that is old and needs replacing?

UNIT **8** How did you react?

1 Think of a time an incident happened to you. Use the ideas below or one of your own.

something went wrong with a cab ride	someone got mad at you
you yelled at someone	you had to get out of a date or appointment
you were late for something	someone was rude to you

2 Prepare your story about the incident to tell the group. What happened? How did you react? How did the people around you react? Think of as many details as you can.

3 **Group work** Take turns telling your stories. Listen to your classmates' stories. Ask questions. Think about what happened and say why. Have you had a similar thing happen to you? Tell the group.

> So one time, I was driving with my friend, and this car was behind us, and the driver was trying to get past us. And he kept honking and flashing his lights. And my friend got really mad and called the police on his cell phone . . .

> The driver behind you must have been in a hurry. He could have been on his way to the hospital.

> Yeah, but he shouldn't have driven like that. It's dangerous.

> I had something like that happen to me one time. . . .

UNIT **10** Quotations

1 **Group work** Look at the quotations below. Do you agree with them? Which one is your favorite?

> A man is a success if he gets up in the morning and gets to bed at night, and in between does what he wants to do.   – Bob Dylan

> Having a lot of money does not automatically make you a successful person. What you want is money and meaning. You want your work to be meaningful, because meaning is what brings the real richness to your life.
> – Oprah Winfrey

> You don't have to be famous. You just have to make your mother and father proud of you.
> – Meryl Streep

> Success is a state of mind. If you want success, start thinking of yourself as a success.
> – Dr. Joyce Brothers

> All you need in this life is ignorance and confidence; then success is sure.
> – Mark Twain

> Success is really about being ready for the good opportunities that come before you.
> – Eric Schmidt

2 Can you think up your own definition of "success"? Complete the sentence below.

Success is _____ .

3 **Class activity** Now go around the class and find out your classmates' definitions. Choose the two you like best, and write them down with your classmates' names. Then share your new "quotations" with the class.

Material things

1 Complete the questions below with your own ideas on the topic of "material things."

Material things

1. Can you imagine life without _____ ?
2. How many _____ do you own?
3. Have you ever bought _____ ?
4. Are you good at _____ ?
5. _____ money?
6. When did you last _____ ?
7. Do you think you'll ever own a _____ ?
8. Do you think people _____ ?

2 **Pair work** Ask and answer your questions. Remember the questions your partner asks.

3 **Pair work** Find a new partner. Tell each other the questions you were asked, and say how you answered them.

"Mario asked me if I could imagine life without the Internet. I told him I had to go without the Internet last weekend, and it was awful!"

UNIT **11** **What's trending?**

1 **Pair work** Look at the topics below. What trends have you noticed in each of these areas? Brainstorm ideas and make a list.

education

lifestyle

communications

entertainment

education
online learning and webinars
more testing

2 **Group work** Join another pair. Discuss the trends on your list. What are they a result of? What impact do you think they will have? Can you predict any trends for the future in these areas?

A *Well, online learning is definitely being introduced into schools in this area.*

B *It's interesting, don't you think? I mean, why is that?*

C *I think it's a result of the demand for more flexible learning opportunities.*

UNIT 12 The best person for the job

1 Look at the different jobs below. Choose a job that you'd like to apply for, and prepare for a job interview. Think of answers to the following questions.

- Why are you interested in this job?
- What experience and qualifications do you have?
- What are your main strengths and weaknesses?
- What qualities do you think someone needs to do this job well?
- Where do you see yourself in five years?

Help Wanted

OFFICE ASSISTANT

Office assistant needed in busy head office of an international trading company. Needs good computer skills and customer service skills.

TUTORS

Tutors needed in English and Math to teach first-year college students who need extra help in these subjects.

STUDENT COUNSELORS

Student counselors needed by foreign student exchange agency to assist students from overseas with all aspects of life in a foreign country.

TECHNOLOGY STAFF

Major technology company needs part-time staff to set up exhibitions around the country, and explain the features of our new products, including cameras and cell phones.

2 **Group work** "Interview" each person for the job they want to apply for. Take turns asking the questions above. At the end of the interview, hold a group vote, and decide if the person should be hired.

"So, Amelie, why are you interested in a job as a student counselor?"

Sounds right

🔊 **4.33** Listen and repeat the words. Notice the underlined sounds. Are the sounds like the sounds in *enjoy*, *choose*, *done*, *serviced*, *straight*, or *there*? Write the words from the list in the correct columns below.

1. adj<u>u</u>st	4. em<u>e</u>rgency	7. n<u>oi</u>se	10. rep<u>ai</u>r
2. c<u>u</u>rtains	5. fl<u>oo</u>ded	8. <u>oi</u>l	11. r<u>ou</u>tine
3. decor<u>a</u>te	6. h<u>ai</u>r	9. p<u>ai</u>nt	12. scr<u>ew</u>driver

enj<u>oy</u>	ch<u>oose</u>	d<u>o</u>ne	serv<u>i</u>ced	str<u>aigh</u>t	th<u>ere</u>
		adjust			

🔊 **4.34** Listen and repeat the pairs of words. Notice the underlined sounds. Are the sounds the same (S) or different (D)? Write *S* or *D*.

1. str<u>e</u>ssed / d<u>ea</u>d __S__

2. em<u>o</u>tional / g<u>o</u>tten ____

3. <u>a</u>ggressive / <u>a</u>ngry ____

4. j<u>ea</u>lous / intel<u>li</u>gent ____

5. <u>sh</u>ould / motiva<u>ti</u>on ____

6. de<u>c</u>isive / di<u>sc</u>ipline ____

7. aggre<u>ss</u>ion / depre<u>ss</u>ed ____

8. <u>sy</u>mpathetic / g<u>ui</u>lty ____

9. c<u>o</u>nfidence / h<u>o</u>nesty ____

UNIT 9

◀)) **4.35** Listen and repeat the words. Underline the silent letter in each word.

1. answer	3. debt	5. honest	7. sign	9. could	11. half
2. budget	4. gadget	6. should	8. walk	10. might	12. listen

UNIT 10

◀)) **4.36** Listen and repeat the words. Notice that one or more syllables in each word are unstressed. They have a weak vowel which sounds like the /ə/ sound in *person*. Circle the weak vowels.

1. album	4. confidence	7. famous	10. recently
2. amazing	5. connections	8. happened	11. seminar
3. career	6. extra	9. millionaire	12. talent

UNIT 11

◀)) **4.37** Listen and repeat the words. Notice the underlined sounds. Which sound in each group is different? Circle the word with the sound that's different.

1. consumption	natural	ocean	shortage
2. congestion	energy	garbage	gas
3. conserve	consume	recycle	rising
4. carbon	outsource	warming	warning
5. change	chemical	packaging	technology
6. because	brought	drought	talk

UNIT 12

◀)) **4.38** Listen and repeat the words. Notice the underlined sounds. Are the sounds like the sounds in *analyst*, *apply*, *construction*, *engineer*, *personality*, or *recruit*? Write the words from the list in the correct columns below.

1. advertising	7. experience
2. business	8. psychiatric
3. choose	9. publishing
4. career	10. research
5. civil	11. surgeon
6. love	12. school

analyst	apply	construction	engineer	personality	recruit
	advertising				

139

Extra practice

Lesson A Causative *get* and *have*

A Complete the sentences. Use the verbs given.

1. I don't have my clothes ___cleaned___ (clean) professionally.
2. We usually have my brother _____ (repair) things around the house.
3. My friends get me _____ (fix) their computer problems.
4. I've never had my hair _____ (color).
5. I often get my sister _____ (cook) for me.
6. My neighbor gets his windows _____ (wash) every week.
7. When I throw a party, I get friends _____ (help) me.
8. I don't have my car _____ (service) regularly.
9. I always get people _____ (help) me when I try to fix anything in the house.
10. I don't buy new shoes very often. I like to get them _____ (repair). In fact, I'm having a pair of boots _____ (repair) right now.

About you **B Pair work** Are the sentences above true for you? How do you get these things done? Discuss with a partner.

Lesson B *need* + passive infinitive and *need* + verb + *-ing*

A Complete the list of things that need doing in Mia's apartment.

- *front door doesn't close — fix the lock*
- *some lights don't work — change the bulbs*
- *large crack in window — replace the glass*
- *shelves in kitchen aren't straight — adjust them*
- *TV making a strange noise — repair it*
- *leaking bathroom faucet — tighten the faucet*
- *dirty rug — clean it*
- *stain on kitchen wall — paint it*

1. The lock needs ___to be fixed / fixing___ .
2. Some bulbs need _____ .
3. The glass in the window needs _____ .
4. The shelves need _____ .
5. The TV needs _____ .
6. The faucet needs _____ .
7. The rug needs _____ .
8. The wall needs _____ .

> **In conversation**
>
> *need* + passive infinitive is more common than *need* + verb + *-ing*.
>
> *need* + verb + *-ing* ▮▮
>
> *need* + passive infinitive ▮▮▮▮▮▮▮▮▮▮▮▮▮▮▮

About you **B Pair work** Do any of the things above need doing in your apartment? Tell a partner. What else needs fixing?

Extra practice

unit

UNIT 8

Lesson A   Past modals *would have*, *should have*, *could have*

A ~~Cross out~~ the incorrect words. Then write answers to the questions.

1. Dan's daughter was sick and couldn't go to school. Dan took her to work with him.
   What <u>could</u> / ~~would~~ he have done instead? _____

2. Ashley had a meal at a restaurant. The food was tasteless, and the service was rude. She complained politely and left. What else <u>could</u> / <u>would</u> she have done? _____

3. There were six cartons of milk left at the grocery store. A man pushed in front of me and picked up all six. I really needed one. <u>Should</u> / <u>Would</u> I have said something? _____

4. Sara borrowed a dress of Kate's. She spilled coffee on it. She gave it back with a stain on it without saying anything. What <u>should</u> / <u>would</u> she have done? _____

5. Josh bought a camera. It should have cost $500, but the salesperson charged him the wrong price of $395. <u>Should</u> / <u>Would</u> Josh have said anything? _____

6. Hal had an important meeting that he hadn't prepared for. He said he wasn't feeling well and went home. <u>Would</u> / <u>Should</u> you have done the same thing? _____

About you   **B** **Pair work** Discuss your answers to the questions above.
Do you have the same views?

> **✗ Common errors**
>
> Use *should have*, not *must have*, + past participle, to talk about the right thing to do.
>
> She **should have** called me.
> (NOT ~~She must have called me.~~)

UNIT 8

Lesson B   Past modals for speculation

A Write a sentence to explain each situation. Start the sentences with the words given. There may be more than one correct answer.

1. You're stuck in a traffic jam, and you're sure there's been an accident.
   "There *must have been an accident*   ."

2. You're in a nice restaurant, and the couple at the table next to you aren't talking to each other. You think it's possible they've had a fight.
   "They _____."

3. You don't think it's possible that you left your credit card at the store.
   "I _____."

4. When you arrive at the dentist for an appointment, they tell you that you are an hour late. You think it's possible you wrote down the wrong time.
   "I _____."

5. You call your sister, but someone else answers. You're sure that you called the wrong number.
   "I _____."

6. Your mother didn't send you a birthday card. It's not possible that she has forgotten.
   "She _____."

About you   **B** **Pair work** Compare your answers. Have you ever been in situations like the ones above?
Share stories.

C **Pair work** Imagine that you're at a coffee shop. You can't find your wallet to pay. Think of as many reasons as you can why this is possible. Tell your partner.

"I must have left my wallet at home."

147

UNIT 9 Lesson A Reported speech

A Read what Pablo says. Then complete the sentences to report what he said.

"I don't think that I'm very materialistic. I'm moving to a new apartment soon, and so I've been trying to get rid of the things I don't want. I actually think I'm very self-disciplined – I only spend money on things I really need. I mean, I've kept a few gifts that I've never used. You know, things that close friends gave to me. And I've kept some old family photos that I can't throw away, obviously. But over the years, I've bought a lot of books, and I'll probably give most of them away."

Note

Present continuous forms in direct speech shift back to past continuous forms in reported speech.

*"**I'm destroying** all my things."* → *He said that he **was destroying** all his things.*

1. Pablo said that he *didn't think* that he _____ very materialistic.

2. He said he _____ to a new apartment, and so he _____ to get rid of the things he _____ .

3. He said he _____ that he _____ very self-disciplined and said he only _____ money on things he really _____ .

4. He said that he _____ a few gifts that he _____ _____ – things that close friends _____ to him.

5. He said he _____ some old family photos that he _____ throw away.

6. He said that over the years, he _____ a lot of books and that he _____ probably give most of them away.

Common errors

Don't use *say* + *me*, *him*, *them*, etc.

She said she wasn't materialistic.
(NOT ~~She said me she wasn't materialistic.~~)

About you **B** Pair work Ask your partner, "Are you materialistic? Could you give away your possessions?" Then find another partner and report the answers.

UNIT 9 Lesson B Reported questions

A Imagine a market researcher asked you these questions. Write the reported questions.

1. Are you saving up for anything special? *He asked me if . . .*
2. How much money have you spent today?
3. What's your favorite store?
4. Could you live without your smartphone?
5. How do you keep track of your money?
6. Does your bank account pay good interest?
7. How often do you check your bank account?
8. Do you ever spend too much on things?

In conversation

*. . . asked **if** and . . . wanted to know **if*** are much more frequent than *. . . asked **whether** and . . . wanted to know **whether**.*

Common errors

Don't use *tell* to report questions.

*She **asked** me if I owned any stocks.*
(NOT ~~She told me if I owned any stocks.~~)

About you **B** Pair work Ask and answer the questions. Then find another partner and report the questions and your first partner's answers.

UNIT 10 Lesson A Talking hypothetically about the past

A These people are talking hypothetically about the past. Complete the sentences.

1. If I _had worked_ (work) harder at school, I might have gotten a better job.
2. If I hadn't quit my job, I _____ (would not meet) my new friends.
3. If my family _____ (not encourage) me, I wouldn't have had the confidence to apply for my current job.
4. If my neighbor _____ (take) different subjects, he would have had better job opportunities.
5. If I'd gotten better grades, I _____ (could get) into grad school.
6. If I had studied English at an earlier age, I _____ (might take) this class years ago.
7. If my parents hadn't set aside the money, they _____ (could not afford) a big house.
8. If we _____ (grow up) 50 years ago, our lives might have been very different.

About you **B** **Pair work** Make four of the sentences above true for you, and tell a partner. Give more information.

"If my friend Robin had worked harder in school, she would have passed more exams and she would have gotten a better job."

UNIT 10 Lesson B Tag questions

A Complete the sentences with a tag question.

1. Celebrity couples often have problems with their marriages, _don't they_ ?
2. People are not really watching reality shows anymore, _____ ? They've lost interest in them.
3. You don't have to have a lot of confidence to go on a talent show, _____ ?
4. It's easier to become an Internet celebrity these days, _____ ?
5. Some actors don't deserve all the bad press they get, _____ ?
6. To be successful in Hollywood, you have to have connections, _____ ?
7. Some singers are just terrible when they perform live, _____ ? I'm not the only one who thinks that, _____ ?
8. The old black and white movies were much better than today's movies, _____ ?
9. Some actors have dropped out of sight completely, _____ ?
10. They're making a lot of violent movies these days, _____ ? I'm right about that, _____ ?

> **i Note**
>
> Notice how to make tag questions when the verb in the statement is *have* or a continuous verb.
>
> *You **have** a guitar, **don't you?***
>
> *She **didn't have** connections, **did she?***
>
> *He**'s doing** really well, **isn't he?***
>
> *They **were getting** bad press, **weren't they?***
>
> Notice how to make tag questions with *I'm . . .* and *I'm not . . .*
>
> *I'm right, **aren't I?***
>
> *I'm not wrong, **am I?***

About you **B** **Pair work** Start conversations with the sentences above. Do you agree? Give your own views.

UNIT **11** **Lesson A** Passive of present continuous and present perfect

A Which of the sentences below need a passive, not an active, verb? Correct the sentences.

being created

1. Fewer jobs are ~~creating~~ in the construction industry.

> **✗ Common errors**
> Don't forget to use the passive when you don't know who is doing the action.
> *More roads **are being built** every year.*
> (NOT ~~More roads are building every year.~~)

2. Fast food chains are providing healthier meals.
3. Skilled workers have recruited from other countries.
4. Smoking has banned in public places.
5. A lot of older houses have knocked down to make room for new buildings.
6. In the last few years, young people haven't encouraged to go to college.
7. Plans to address water shortages have not discussed.
8. More and more life-saving medicines have developed in the last ten years.
9. A large number of bank employees have laid off because their jobs have outsourced to other countries.
10. New gyms and swimming pools are building in some neighborhoods because people are demanding better facilities.

About you **B** **Pair work** Which of the sentences above are true where you live? Discuss with a partner.

UNIT **11** **Lesson B** Linking ideas

A Rewrite the sentences using the expressions given.

1. I think it's better to get around by bicycle than to drive your car everywhere. (instead of)
   I think it's better to get around by bicycle instead of driving your car everywhere.

2. I'm concerned that carbon dioxide levels are rising because of increased burning of fuels. (due to)

3. I'm worried that congestion on the roads is still a problem, even though there have been improvements. (in spite of)

4. It's annoying that people often throw away plastic bottles when you can recycle them. (even though)

5. I think we should use things like lemon juice as a cleaning product – then we won't need to buy so many toxic chemicals. (so that)

6. We should reduce our energy use so we can protect the environment. (in order to)

7. It worries me that obesity in children is becoming more of a problem because of unhealthy eating habits. (as a result of)

About you **B** **Pair work** Do you agree with any of the concerns above? Brainstorm solutions to the problems.

Lesson A *What* clauses and long noun phrases as subjects

A Rewrite these sentences to give someone advice about starting a new job. Start with the words given.

1. Making a good impression is really important.

   What _____ .

2. A friend of mine offered to help the manager.

   Something _____ .

3. My sister introduced herself to everyone.

   What _____ .

4. Smile – that's the best thing you can do.

   The _____ .

5. I would try to listen and learn from your co-workers.

   What _____ .

6. I like to find out as much about the job as possible before starting. Then you feel prepared.

   What _____ .

   The advantage of that _____ .

B **Pair work** Do you agree with this advice? What other advice do you have for someone on their first day at work?

Lesson B The future continuous and future perfect

A Read what Natalie says about her future. Then complete the sentences.

"I'm finishing my degree in math right now. I hope I do well on my exams because I've applied to go to medical school next year. The program lasts four years, and then there are three to seven years of internship to do after that. I don't know what type of medicine I want to work in yet, but I have a lot of time to decide. I might go and work in another country. Who knows?"

1. In a few months, Natalie _____ (finish) her degree in math, and she _____ (get) ready to go to medical school.

2. Five years after that, she _____ (leave) medical school, and she _____ (do) an internship somewhere.

3. She probably _____ (not decide) which area of medicine she'd like to work in by then.

4. She doesn't know who she _____ (work) with or where she _____ (live).

5. She _____ (might move) to a different country to work.

B **Pair work** Think of three ideas for each question. Tell your partner.

What will you be doing . . .

- 24 hours from now?
- in three months?
- in five years?

What will you have done by then?

Illustration credits

Harry Briggs: 7, 31, 55, 68, 69, 95   **Bunky Hurter:** 14, 36, 54, 77, 100   **Scott Macneil:** 71   **Q2A studio artists:** 24, 47, 57, 79, 89   **Lucy Truman:** 10, 20, 30, 42, 52, 62, 74, 84, 94, 106, 116, 126

Photography credits

Back cover: ©vovan/Shutterstock   **38, 39, 58, 59, 90, 91, 112, 113** ©Cambridge University Press   **6, 7, 12, 26, 27, 70, 71, 80, 102, 103, 118, 122, 123** ©Frank Veronsky   **viii** *(left to right)* ©RubberBall/SuperStock; ©Cultura Limited/SuperStock   **1** *(clockwise from top left)* ©Marmaduke St. John/Alamy; ©Exactostock/SuperStock; ©Nicola Tree/Getty Images; ©Steven Robertson/istockphoto   **2** ©Thinkstock; *(top background)* ©monticello/Shutterstock   **3** ©Masterfile/RF   **4** ©blackred/istockphoto; *(background)* ©ruskpp/Shutterstock   **8** ©Jordan Strauss/Invision/AP; *(utensils)* ©Martin Kemp/Shutterstock   **9** ©2010 AFP/Getty Images   **11** *(clockwise from top left)* ©Blend Images/SuperStock; ©Radius/SuperStock; ©Transtock/SuperStock; ©Blend Images/SuperStock   **12** *(all photos)* ©Frank Veronsky   **13** ©Thomas Barwick/Getty Images   **15** *(all photos)* ©Cambridge University Press   **16** ©Imagemore/SuperStock   **17** ©Imagemore/SuperStock   **18** *(left to right)* ©quavondo/Getty Images; ©Dreampictures/Media Bakery   **21** *(clockwise from top left)* ©Pixtal/SuperStock; ©miker/Shutterstock.com; ©Pixtal/SuperStock; ©Steve Vidler/SuperStock; ©Pacific Stock - Design Pics/SuperStock; ©windmoon/Shutterstock.com   **22** *(clockwise from top left)* ©Gregory Johnston/age fotostock/SuperStock; ©Linzy Slusher/istockphoto; ©Thinkstock; ©Juanmonino/Getty Images; ©Thinkstock; ©Kerrie Kerr/istockphoto; ©Steve Kaufman/CORBIS; ©Marco Maccarini/istockphoto   **25** ©Bill Sykes Images/Getty Images   **28** *(background)* ©Shutterstock   **29** *(all backgrounds)* ©Shutterstock   **32** *(top to bottom)* ©Blend Images/SuperStock; ©4kodiak/istockphoto   **33** *(clockwise from top left)* ©Chris Whitehead/Getty Images; ©Thinkstock; ©Thinkstock; ©PYMCA/SuperStock   **34** *(clockwise from top left)* ©Thinkstock; ©Fancy Collection/SuperStock; ©Thinkstock; ©Jupiterimages/Thinkstock; ©Edward Bock/istockphoto; ©Mie Ahmt/istockphoto; ©Exactostock/SuperStock; ©Silvia Jansen/istockphoto   **35** ©Image Source/SuperStock   **40** *(hole)* ©Fotana/Shutterstock   **41** ©Nicole S. Young/istockphoto   **43** *(clockwise from top right)* ©Transtock/SuperStock; ©Thinkstock; ©Exactostock/SuperStock   **44** *(clockwise from top left)* ©Thinkstock; ©Thinkstock; ©Jupiterimages/Thinkstock; ©Jupiterimages/Thinkstock; ©Thinkstock   **48** *(people)* ©Blaj Gabriel/Shutterstock *(bus stop)* ©Joy Rector/Shutterstock *(sign)* ©Rob Wilson/Shutterstock   **49** *(top)* ©Blaj Gabriel/Shutterstock *(bottom)* ©Jack Hollingsworth/Getty Images   **50** ©Olivier Lantzendörffer/istockphoto; *(background)* ©Hluboki Dzianis/Shutterstock   **51** *(background)* ©Hluboki Dzianis/Shutterstock   **53** *(clockwise from top left)* ©The Power of Forever Photography/istockphoto; ©PhotoAlto/SuperStock; ©Thinkstock; ©Thinkstock; ©Ingram Publishing/SuperStock   **54** *(left to right)* ©Paul Hakimata/Fotolia; ©Jupiterimages/Thinkstock   **56** *(top section, top to bottom)* ©Eric Isselee/Shutterstock; ©Flavia Morlachetti/Shutterstock; ©Eric Isselee/Shutterstock; ©ULKASTUDIO/Shutterstock; ©Coprid/Shutterstock *(bottom row, left to right)* ©Morgan Lane Photography/Shutterstock; ©Peter Waters/Shutterstock; ©Eric Isselee/Shutterstock; ©Yu Lan/Shutterstock; (background) ©sunil menon/istockphoto   **60** Photo Courtesy of Mary E. Holmes   **63** *(left to right)* ©Arcady/Shutterstock; ©Arcady/Shutterstock; ©Miguel Angel Salinas Salinas/Shutterstock; ©Arcady/Shutterstock; ©Olga Anourina/istockphoto   **64** ©altrendo images/Getty Images   **65** *(clockwise from top left)* ©Yuri Arcurs Media/SuperStock; ©Exactostock/SuperStock; ©Niels Busch/Getty Images; ©Blend Images/SuperStock; ©baranq/Shutterstock; ©moodboard/SuperStock   **66** *(clockwise from top left)* ©Michael Hitoshi/Getty Images; ©Jupiterimages/Thinkstock; ©Catherine Yeulet/istockphoto; ©Jupiterimages/Getty Images   **67** *(invitation)* ©mark wragg/istockphoto *(photographer)* ©Marcin Stefaniak/istockphoto *(cake)* ©Dean Turner/istockphoto *(dress)* ©fStop/SuperStock *(flowers)* ©RubberBall/SuperStock   ©Lana Sundman/age fotostock/SuperStock   **73** ©Dfree/Shutterstock   **75** *(clockwise from top left)* ©Thinkstock; ©Thinkstock; ©Thinkstock; ©Photo and Co/Getty Images   **76** ©digitalskillet/istockphoto   **81** ©BanksPhotos/istockphoto   **82** ©Michael Rosenwirth/Alamy; *(background)* ©argus/Shutterstock   **85** *(clockwise from top right)* ©Thinkstock; ©Jamie Grill/Getty Images; ©Fotosearch/SuperStock; ©Dmitry Kalinovsky/istockphoto   **86** *(top, left to right)* ©WireImage/Getty Images; ©Julian Stallabrass/Flickr; *(bottom)* ©Photocrea/Shutterstock   **88** *(background)* © photolinc/Shutterstock   **91** ©Bruce Glikas/Getty Images   **92** ©stevecoleimages/istockphoto; *(background)* ©Loskutnikov/Shutterstock   **97** *(clockwise from bottom left)* ©Getty Images; ©Indigo/Getty Images; ©Getty Images; ©GYI NSEA/istockphoto; ©GYI NSEA/istockphoto   **98** *(top to bottom)* ©Featureflash/Shutterstock.com; ©Thinkstock; ©Ciaran Griffin/Thinkstock; ©Comstock Images/Thinkstock; *(background)* ©Henning Riemer/Shutterstock   **99** ©Paul A. Hebert/Getty Images   **101** *(top to bottom)* ©Getty Images; ©Time & Life Pictures/Getty Images   **104** *(left to right)* ©GYI NSEA/istockphoto; ©Featureflash/Shutterstock.com; ©GYI NSEA/istockphoto   **107** *(clockwise from top left)* ©Edward Bock/istockphoto; ©TIM MCCAIG/istockphoto; ©Johner/SuperStock; ©Thinkstock   **108** *(top row, left to right)* ©Thinkstock; ©Comstock Images/Thinkstock; ©Thinkstock *(bottom row, all photos)* ©Thinkstock   **110** ©Thinkstock   **114** *(top to bottom)* ©Debby Wong/Shutterstock.com; ©Stockbyte/Thinkstock; *(background)* ©Itana/Shutterstock   **115** ©Thinkstock; *(background)* ©Itana/Shutterstock   **117** *(clockwise from top left)* ©Jack Hollingsworth/Thinkstock; ©Andrew Rich/istockphoto; ©Alexander Podshivalov/istockphoto; ©Blend Images/SuperStock   **120** *(clockwise from top left)* ©Thinkstock; ©ViviSuArt/istockphoto; ©Neustockimages/istockphoto; ©Don Bayley/istockphoto; ©Thinkstock   **124** ©age fotostock/SuperStock   **128** *(left to right)* ©Rich Legg/istockphoto; ©daniel rodriguez/istockphoto; ©Stephanie Swartz/istockphoto   **130** *(left to right)* ©Martijn Mulder/istockphoto; ©Corbis/SuperStock   **131** ©Oliver Gutfleisch/ima/imagebroker.net/SuperStock   **132** ©Ghislain & Marie David de Lossy/Getty Images   **134** ©Monkey Business Images/Shutterstock   **135** *(clockwise from top left)* ©hxdbzxy/Shutterstock; ©Sandra Baker/Alamy; ©bikeriderlondon/Shutterstock; ©ArtFamily/Shutterstock   **136** *(background)* ©Gunnar Pippel/Shutterstock   **141** *(top to bottom)* ©Thinkstock; ©Thinkstock; ©Lorraine Kourafas/Shutterstock; ©Chamille White/Shutterstock   **145** ©Jupiterimages/Thinkstock

Text credits

The authors and publishers acknowledge the following sources of copyright material and are grateful for the permissions granted. While every effort has been made, it has not always been possible to identify the sources of all the material used, or to trace all copyright holders. If any omissions are brought to our notice, we will be happy to include the appropriate acknowledgments on reprinting.

8 Text adapted from "Blind Chef Christine Ha Crowned 'MasterChef' in Finale" by Ryan Owens and Meredith Frost, *ABC News*, September 11, 2012. Reproduced with permission of ABC News.

40 Quotes from *Quiet: The Power of Introverts in a World That Can't Stop Talking* by Susan Cain, Penguin Books, 2012. Copyright ©Susan Cain. Reproduced by permission of Penguin Books Ltd.

SECOND EDITION

TOUCHSTONE

WORKBOOK 4B

MICHAEL McCARTHY

JEANNE McCARTEN

HELEN SANDIFORD

CAMBRIDGE
UNIVERSITY PRESS

Contents

1 He's the guy . . .

Grammar | Choose the correct relative pronoun to complete each sentence. If a relative pronoun is not needed, circle the dash (—).

1. This is Andrew. He's the guy **which** / ⊝ I met on vacation in Florida.

2. This is the dog **that / who** followed me on the beach one day. It turned out to be Andrew's dog. So I guess it was the dog **that / —** introduced us.

3. This is the amusement park **who / —** we went to on our first date. And this is the ticket for the first movie **that / who** we saw.

4. Here's the necklace **that / who** he gave me before I left for home. Andrew is someone **which / who** I'm going to keep in touch with.

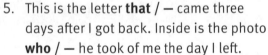

5. This is the letter **that / —** came three days after I got back. Inside is the photo **who / —** he took of me the day I left.

6. We talk every day. And this is the phone bill **who / that** I got yesterday!

2 She's the girl . . .

Grammar | Complete the email with *who*, *that*, or *which*. Put the word in parentheses ( ) if the sentence is also complete without the relative pronoun. Sometimes more than one answer is possible.

New Message

To: mel_bes@cup.com
From: camilleS@cup.com
Subject: Estella and Ramiro

Dear Melania,

I'm so excited about some news _(that / which)_ I just got from a friend. You know Estella, right? She's my friend from Peru _____ I met in college. Well, last year I introduced her to that cute guy, Ramiro, _____ I used to work with. He had the desk _____ was across from mine. Anyway, a group of us used to go out together sometimes after work. One day, I invited Estella along. (I knew Ramiro was exactly the kind of guy _____ she would like.) We went to the Caribbean restaurant _____ I love on Essex Street. To make a long story short, they met that night, and now they're getting married. I just got the invitation. I can't wait for the wedding!

Camille

3 I have a friend . . .

Grammar | Use the sentences in the box and *who*, *that*, or *which* to complete the sentences below. Put the relative pronoun in parentheses ( ) if the sentence is also complete without it. Sometimes more than one answer is possible.

Her family owns a store.	It served traditional Korean food.	The paper has rose petals in it.
I spoke to her in Korean.	✓She lives in South Korea.	The shop sells handmade paper.

1. I have a friend, Seung-Li, _who / that lives in South Korea_____ .
2. I met her in Seoul at the store _____ .
3. It is a very special shop _____ .
4. I bought some paper _____ .
5. She was the only person _____ .
6. Later, she invited me to a restaurant _____ .

4 About you

Grammar | Complete the sentences with true information. Use relative pronouns where necessary.

1. I have a friend _who speaks three languages_____ .
2. My neighbor is someone _____ .
3. I like stores _____ .
4. I take a class _____ .
5. I don't like the food _____ .
6. I know someone _____ .

1 Which particle?

Grammar and vocabulary | Circle the correct particle to complete each sentence.

1. My sister's not home. She went **up** / **away** / **along** for the weekend.
2. I grew **out** / **down** / **up** in Morocco, but now I live in California.
3. My brother isn't ready to settle **out** / **up** / **down**. He doesn't want to get married yet.
4. My mother's away on business now, but she plans to fly **away** / **along** / **back** next Tuesday.
5. I thought I had a doctor's appointment today, but it turns **out** / **up** / **down** that it's next week.
6. My best friend is moving **up** / **away** / **along** next month. I'm going to miss her.
7. I forgot to sign **back** / **out** / **up** for the class trip to the museum, so I can't go.
8. I sent my cousin an email last week, but he never wrote **back** / **away** / **out**.

2 Figure it out!

Grammar and vocabulary | Complete the sentences with the phrasal verbs in the box. Then complete the puzzle and the sentence below.

come back	go away	sign up	✓ write back
get along	grow up	work out	

1. When a friend sends you an email, you should _write back_ immediately.
2. If a relationship doesn't _____ , don't worry about it. It may be for the best.
3. If you want to _____ well with someone, be a good friend!
4. It's good to take a break from your usual routine and _____ for a few days.
5. It's fun to go on vacation, but it's always good to _____ home, too!
6. A lot of kids _____ in blended families these days.
7. One way to meet new people is to _____ for a class.

1. w r i t e | b | a c k
2. ___ ___ | | ___ ___ ___ ___
3. ___ | | ___ ___ ___ ___ ___ ___
4. ___ ___ | | ___ ___ ___ ___
5. ___ ___ ___ ___ ___ | |
6. ___ ___ ___ | |
7. ___ ___ ___ ___ ___ | |

Some couples like to _____ _____ because they think it's fun to make up and get back together!

3 Breaking up is hard to do.

Grammar
and
vocabulary Complete the conversation with the correct form of the phrasal verbs in the box.
Sometimes more than one answer is possible.

| ✓ break up | go out | turn out |
| get along | hang out | work out |

Tina   Hi, Jorge. You don't look so good. What's wrong?

Jorge   Well, my girlfriend and I _broke up_ last week.

Tina   Oh, no. You did? That's too bad. How long were
you _____ with her?

Jorge   About three months. I can't believe things
didn't _____ . I mean, we _____
really well. I thought everything was fine.

Tina   Yeah, you guys were always _____
together.

Jorge   I know. We saw each other almost every day!

Tina   Well, maybe that was the problem. Maybe she
didn't want to spend every minute of every day with you.

Jorge   Yeah, I guess you're right. Things didn't _____ the way
I thought.

Tina   Why don't you talk to her? Ask her what she wants in a relationship.

4 About you

Grammar
and
vocabulary Answer the questions with true information.

1. Who do you get along well with? Why?
   I get along well with my sister because we are very similar.

2. Do you like to go away for summer vacation?
   _____

3. Where do you and your friends like to hang out?
   _____

4. Do you always write back immediately when someone sends you an email?
   _____

5. Are there any classes you would like to sign up for?
   _____

6. Do you think you'll ever move far away from home?
   _____

1 I guess . . .

Conversation strategies **Rewrite each sentence with the two "softening" expressions in parentheses to complete the conversations.**

1. **A** What's wrong with Jamil? He just yelled at me for turning on the TV.

   B _He's probably just tired._ He stayed
   He's tired. (probably / just)

   up all night. He had to finish a paper for school.

   A He always waits until the last minute to do his work.

   B I know. _____
   He's disorganized. (I guess / kind of)

   A Yeah, and he has so many activities at school.

   _____
   He's doing too much. (I think / a bit)

   B But it's good to be involved with your school.

   A That's true. _____
   He's stressed out. (I guess / sort of)

2. **A** Have you met Alissa yet? She's the new student in our class.

   B Yeah. I talked to her yesterday, but she didn't say much.

   A _____
   She's shy. (maybe / just)

   B Yeah, I'm sure she'll meet people soon.

   _____
   It takes time. (just / a little)

   A It's difficult when you don't know anyone.

   B I know. _____
   It's hard to fit in. (I think / sort of)

   A Yeah. _____
   Making friends is hard. (I guess / in a way)

2 It's spicy, though.

Conversation
strategies Complete the conversations with the responses in the box.
Add *though* if appropriate.

> He's pretty shy.   I'll find out when he's free.
> He's here for two weeks.   It was a little spicy.
> ✓ I love Thai food.   It was really nice.

1. Lee   How was your dinner date last night?

    Kyra Great. We went to a Thai restaurant that Wayne knows.

    Lee   Cool. *I love Thai food.* _____ What did you have?

    Kyra Green curry with chicken and a vegetable dish.

    Lee   Was it good?

    Kyra Yeah, the food was excellent. _____

          I don't usually like spicy food, but I really enjoyed it.

    Lee   Was it expensive?

    Kyra Well, it was a little expensive. _____

2. Becky Brad, who's the new guy in your department?

    Brad   Oh, that's Bart. He's just visiting from the Los Angeles

           office. _____

    Becky Only two weeks? That's too bad. He seems interesting.

    Brad   Yeah. _____ He's probably kind of lonely.

    Becky Well, maybe we should invite him to dinner. Then we

           could show him around a little before he leaves.

    Brad   That sounds like a great idea. _____

3 About you

Conversation
strategies Use true information to answer each set of questions. Respond to the
first question using "softening" comments. Then respond to the second
question using *though*.

1. What's something you're bad at? What's something you're good at?
    I guess I'm kind of bad at playing tennis. I'm really great at playing chess, though.

2. What's your worst quality? What's your best quality?

    _____

3. What's difficult about learning English? What do you like about learning English?

    _____

4. What annoying habit does one of your friends have? What's nice about him or her?

    _____

5. What's your least favorite kind of music? What's your favorite kind?

    _____

1 Interactive communities

Reading | **A Read the article. What topics are discussed? Check (✓) all that apply.**

☐ dating sites   ☐ meeting people offline   ☐ phone apps   ☐ social networking

Using the online world to go offline

With our ability to connect to almost anyone in the world at any time, are we feeling more alone than ever? That's the question that critics of technology are asking. Some research suggests that people who use the Internet and social networks a lot often feel isolated and lonelier than people who don't. Supporters of online socializing disagree and point out that it's up to the user whether or not an online relationship becomes a meaningful, face-to-face one. After all, social networks, Internet companies, and app developers are merely doing their job – connecting users online. The next steps from online to offline are for us, the users, to take.

In fact, social networking websites often give us all the tools we need to move easily from an online relationship to an offline one. For example, there are websites that organize groups around particular interests. Perhaps you've just moved to a new city and want to meet people who have the same interests as you. You can sign up on websites that help you find others who enjoy the same hobbies. Many of these groups

plan face-to-face activities. It's a great way to connect with people you would never meet otherwise. There's no guarantee that you'll get along, but at least you'll have something in common.

Apps for cell phones or tablets can also help us connect with people offline in several ways. Some apps let you find friends nearby, find out what they are doing, and who's available to hang out. Other apps help you plan activities. You can send an invitation to friends electronically and include details about the activity, maps, and directions for how to get there. The people you invite can respond in the same way. There are also apps that recommend where you can meet people, for example, at restaurants or museums.

Technology doesn't have to isolate us. There are plenty of websites and phone apps that help us create social networks, both online and in real life. The trick is to make the effort. At some point, we have to pull our attention away from the screen in order to actually meet someone.

B Read the article again. Are the sentences true, false, or is the information not given? Write *T* (true), *F* (false), or *D* (doesn't say).

1. People who spend too much time online can feel lonely. __*T*__

2. The writer suggests that social networks are to blame for people's loneliness. ____

3. Websites that are for people with similar interests connect people that get along. ____

4. If you sign up for a website that organizes face-to-face activities, you'll meet new people that you like. ____

5. Most people only want to use websites and apps to find dates, not to find friends. ____

6. Technology can improve your relationships with your circle of friends. ____

2 Common ground

Writing **A** Read the email. Then complete the sentences with *both*, *both of us*, or *neither of us*.

New Message

To: mitch_88@cup.com
From: PhilJ@cup.com
Subject: Your high school friend

Dear Mitch,

Remember me from high school? I'm the guy who sat behind you in world literature class. I got your email address from Kurt, the guy we ___*both*___ used to hang out with at lunchtime.

I'll always remember that class. _____ hated reading those short stories, but we had to take the class for some reason. And _____ liked our teacher, Mr. What's-his-name. He wasn't a very good teacher at all. It's amazing that we _____ passed the final exam. Good thing we _____ stayed up late studying the night before.

Anyway, I was talking to Kurt last week, and _____ would like to see you again. Maybe we can all meet and go out for dinner or something one day soon.

Take care,
Phil

B Write an email to an old friend you haven't seen in a long time. Include things you did and didn't have in common.

New Message

To: buddy1@cup.com
From: buddy2@cup.com
Subject: Long time no see!

_____

_____

_____

_____

Unit 7 Progress chart

What can you do? Mark the boxes. ✓ = I can . . . ? = I need to review how to . . .	To review, go back to these pages in the Student's Book.
Grammar ☐ write sentences with subject and object relative clauses. ☐ use phrasal verbs like *grow up*, *get along*, and *break up*.	66 and 67 68 and 69
Vocabulary ☐ use at least 12 phrasal verbs.	68 and 69
Conversation strategies ☐ use at least 6 expressions to soften comments. ☐ give a contrasting idea using *though*.	70 71
Writing ☐ use *both*, *both of us*, and *neither of us*.	73

When you wish . . .

Grammar | **A** What are these people wishing for right now? Complete the sentences.

1. James _wishes he had a new car_ .

2. Emi and Sue _____ .

3. Joey _____ .

4. Esteban and Pilar _____ .

5. Al _____ .

6. Li-ming _____ .

B Complete the sentences about the people in part A.

1. If James _____had_____ (have) more money, he __would buy__ (buy) a new car.

2. If Emi and Sue _____ (live) in a bigger apartment, they _____ (have) more space.

3. If Joey _____ (be) taller, he _____ (score) more points.

4. If Esteban and Pilar _____ (have) two TVs, they _____ (not have) to watch the same TV shows.

5. If Al _____ (not be) a bad cook, he _____ (eat) better.

6. If Li-ming _____ (live) in the country, she _____ (be) much happier.

2 About you

Grammar | Write true sentences about your wishes.

My Wish List

1. I wish I _had more free time during the week_ . (have)
   If I _had more free time during the week, I'd exercise more_ . (have)

2. I wish I _____ . (be)
   If I _____ . (be)

3. I wish I _____ . (can)
   If I _____ . (can)

4. I wish I _____ . (not be)
   If I _____ . (not be)

5. I wish my parents _____ . (not be)
   If they _____ . (not be)

6. I wish my friend _____ . (be)
   If he or she _____ . (be)

7. I wish I _____ . (have)
   If I _____ . (have)

8. I wish I _____ . (not have to)
   If I _____ . (not have to)

9. I wish I _____ . (live)
   If I _____ . (live)

1 If I had a problem, . . .

Vocabulary | Circle the correct word to complete each sentence. Then decide if each sentence is true or false for you. Write *T* (true) or *F* (false). Correct the false statements.

1. __F__ If I had a problem, I would talk **for** / (**to**)/ **about** my best friend.
   If I had a problem, I would talk to my Aunt Lisa.

2. ____ I always apologize **about** / **to** / **for** my mistakes.
   _____

3. ____ My friends never thank me **for** / **about** / **with** helping them.
   _____

4. ____ I always worry **for** / **about** / **from** taking tests!
   _____

5. ____ I often share books **to** / **with** / **about** my neighbors.
   _____

6. ____ If I forgot **with** / **from** / **about** a friend's birthday, I would feel bad.
   _____

2 Remind me about it.

Vocabulary | Complete the conversations with the words in the box.

ask for	✓forget about	remind about	worry about
borrow from	lend to	talk to	
buy for	pay for	think about	

1. A Where's Marissa? I hope she didn't __*forget*__ __*about*__ our party.

   B I know. Let's call her and _____ her _____ it.

2. A Oh, no. I forgot my wallet. Can I _____ some money _____ you for lunch?

   B Oh, don't _____ _____ it. I'll get lunch. It's my treat!

3. A Do you think I should _____ this camera _____ my sister's birthday?

   B Why don't you _____ _____ her about it first?

4. A Can you _____ ten dollars _____ Lenny to buy a movie ticket?

   B I'm sorry. I can't. I have just enough to _____ _____ my own ticket.

5. A I think we're lost. Should we _____ someone _____ directions to the museum?

   B Not yet. I'm sure if I _____ _____ it for a minute, I'll remember how to get there.

3 ▶ Would you ask for an autograph?

Grammar | **Complete the questions with the correct form of the verbs.**

1. What _would you say_ (say) if you ___met___ (meet) a famous athlete?
   Would you ask (ask) for an autograph?

2. If you _____ (see) an accident, what _____ (do)?
   _____ (call) for an ambulance?

3. What _____ (do) if you _____ (have) a large spider
   on your leg? _____ (scream)?

4. If you _____ (break) your best friend's camera, how
   _____ (feel)? _____ (offer) to replace it?

5. How _____ (react) if your best friend _____ (win)
   a trip to Hawai'i? _____ (feel) jealous?

6. What _____ (say) to your neighbors if they
   _____ (complain) about your music? _____ (apologize)?

4 ▶ About you

Grammar | **Answer the questions in Exercise 3. Write true information.**

1. _If I met a famous athlete, I'd say, "I really admire you!"_
   I would definitely ask for an autograph.
   _____

2. _____
   _____
   _____

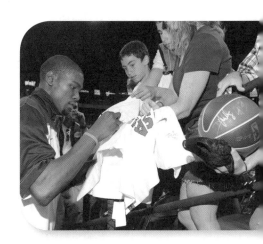

3. _____
   _____
   _____

4. _____
   _____
   _____

5. _____
   _____
   _____

6. _____
   _____

1   I'd choose . . .

<blockquote>
Conversation strategies
</blockquote>

Complete the conversation with the expressions in the box. Sometimes more than one answer is possible.

✓ if I were you, I'd	I would	I wouldn't	you could	you might want to

Serge   I really want to take a vacation this summer, but I need to work, too.

Nina   Well, *if I were you, I'd* take a vacation first. You might not get another chance.

Serge   Hmm. Maybe I should. Where's a good place to go – any ideas?

Nina   Well, there are so many great places. I mean, _____ go anywhere. Have you been to Europe?

Serge   No. I'd love to. It's kind of expensive, though.

Nina   Well, _____ let that stop you! Seriously, you can always get a job there. There are programs for students who want to work abroad. _____ find out about them if I were you.

Serge   I never thought of that.

Nina   _____ look on the Internet and do a little research.

Serge   Yeah. That's a great idea. So, I could work *and* take a vacation.

2   Good advice

<blockquote>
Conversation strategies
</blockquote>

Grace is having a bad day. Respond to her statements with advice.

1. **Grace**   I didn't do very well on my math exam.
   You   *If I were you, I'd talk to the teacher.*

2. **Grace**   Ouch! I just got a bad paper cut.
   You   _____

3. **Grace**   Oh, no! My car won't start.
   You   _____

4. **Grace**   I just stained my favorite sweater.
   You   _____

3 You might want to . . .

Conversation strategies | Look at the pictures. Complete the advice.

1 You look tired. _I would get some coffee_ .

2 The sun's really strong. I _____ _____ .

3 It's very windy. If _____ _____ .

4 It's very cold. You _____ _____ .

4 That would be fun.

Conversation strategies | Respond to each sentence with *That would be* and an appropriate adjective.

1. I'd really like to hike in the Himalayas.

   Wow. That would be awesome!

2. Maybe we could go to the mall this afternoon.

   _____

3. It would be great to win a million dollars.

   _____

4. One day, I'm going to learn to tango.

   _____

1 What do you regret?

Reading | **A** Read the article about regrets. According to the article, which of the following factors affect how people regret things in life?

☐ age ☐ climate ☐ culture ☐ gender ☐ health ☐ income

Regrets? Too few to mention

Do you ever lie awake at night with regrets? Do you spend hours wishing you could change your life? __5__ If so, you're not alone. Regret – that negative feeling you have after a bad experience – is a fairly common human emotion. However, recent research suggests that while almost everyone experiences regret at some point or another, it is much more negative for some than for others.

What do we regret? According to research, we tend to regret decisions we made about our education, careers, romance, and parenting. We feel bad about things we did. ____ We wish we had different life opportunities, could make different choices, and relive moments with different outcomes. However, the nature and impact of regrets can vary across ages, sex, and cultures.

From the research, it would seem that the most striking difference in how regret affects people is between younger and older people. Younger people tend to regret the things they actually did, whereas older people regret the things they didn't do – their missed opportunities. Older people experience regret much more negatively. ____ Younger people are more likely to see a bad

experience as an important learning opportunity. They realize they made a mistake, and they use that to guide their decisions in the future. Older people don't feel they have the same chance to correct their actions and their outcomes.

Gender and culture can also affect what and how we regret. ____ According to some research, more women may regret lost romantic opportunities and family conflicts. More men may regret their decisions around career, money, and education. In cultures that put a high value on personal choice, such as the United States, people tend to have more regrets. In cultures where the family or the community makes more decisions, people have fewer regrets. Research suggests that the more choices we have, the more possibilities we have to regret.

So, if you find yourself staring at the ceiling at 3 a.m., what can you do to turn your regret into something positive? Use it to make better choices in the future. Realize that you couldn't control everything in the past situation. Take more chances in the future. ____ And be a little easier on yourself.

B Read the article again. Then add these missing sentences to the article by writing each number in the correct blank.

1. The differences between men and women are interesting.

2. We may feel worse about the things we didn't do.

3. Have more fun.

4. It can even lead to depression in some older people.

5. Do you torture yourself thinking about your mistakes?

C Choose the correct options to complete the sentences.

1. Feeling regret is **not common** / (**normal**).
2. The feeling of regret is **worse for some** / **the same for everyone**.
3. Older people mostly regret things they **did** / **didn't do**.
4. **Younger** / **Older** people feel they are in a better position to avoid the same mistakes.
5. Regret is **more** / **less** common when people make their own decisions.
6. The article suggests that in the end, regret is **useless** / **useful**.

2 If I won the lottery, . . .

Writing **A** Read the journal entry. Complete the sentences with the adverbs given and the correct verb forms.

> If I won the lottery, I __'d definitely quit__ (definitely / quit) my job, and
> I _____ (probably / not work) at all! If I were a millionaire,
> I _____ (definitely / buy) a house on the beach and one in the
> mountains. If I had two houses, I _____ (definitely / invite) my
> family and friends to visit, but I _____ (probably / not invite)
> them every weekend. I'd want some time for myself. If I had more time for myself, I'd
> write more, and I _____ (probably / try) to publish a book.
> What would the title of the book be? "How to Live Like a Millionaire," of course!

B Write a journal entry about what you would do if you were a millionaire. Use *definitely* and *probably* to show degrees of certainty.

_____

_____

_____

Unit 8 Progress chart

What can you do? Mark the boxes. ✓ = I can . . . ? = I need to review how to . . .	To review, go back to these pages in the Student's Book.
Grammar — ☐ use *wish* + past form of verb for wishes about the present or future.	76 and 77
☐ use *If* + past form of verb, followed by *would* / *could* + verb to talk about imaginary situations in the present or future.	76, 77, and 79
Vocabulary — ☐ use the correct preposition after at least 12 verbs.	78
Conversation strategies — ☐ give advice using expressions like *If I were you* and *You could*.	80
☐ use *That would be* to comment on a possibility or a suggestion.	81
Writing — ☐ use *definitely* and *probably* to show degrees of certainty.	83

Lesson A / Tech support

1 I have no idea why . . .

Grammar | **A Unscramble the questions.**

1. which battery / Do you know / should / buy / I / ?
   Do you know which battery I should buy?

2. they / where / are / Can you tell me / ?
   _____

3. when / you / Can you remember / it / last changed / ?
   _____

4. it / Do you have any idea / how much / costs / ?
   _____

B Unscramble the statements.

1. why / isn't / I have no idea / working / it
   _____

2. last changed it / when / I don't know / I
   _____

3. two / I / if / I wonder / should / batteries / buy
   _____

C Complete the conversation with the questions and statements from parts A and B.

Woman Excuse me. Can you help me?

Clerk Sure. What seems to be the problem?

Woman It's my camera. _I have no idea why it isn't working._

Clerk Hmm. Let me look at it. It might be the battery. _____

Woman No, I can't. _____ I'm not sure if I've ever changed it.

Clerk Well, you definitely need a new one.

Woman _____

Clerk You need a 3.7 volt battery.

Woman _____

Clerk They're $39.99 each.

Woman Great. _____

Clerk Sure. They're at the back of the store. Here, let me show you.

Woman Thanks. _____ Maybe I should have an extra one.

Clerk That might be a good idea.

2 I wonder . . .

Grammar **A** Tara wants to download some music from the Internet. Rewrite the questions she wants to ask her friend Kwang.

1. Can you download songs from this website?
2. How do you put them on your phone?
3. Is there a charge for each song?
4. Can you buy just one song?
5. How do you pay for the songs?
6. How do you make a playlist?
7. Are there any free songs?
8. Can I put the songs on my tablet, too?

1. I wonder *if you can download songs from this website* _____ .
2. Can you tell me _____ ?
3. Do you know _____ ?
4. Do you have any idea _____ ?
5. Do you know _____ ?
6. Can you remember _____ ?
7. I wonder _____ .
8. Do you know _____ ?

B Kwang doesn't know the answers to Tara's questions. Write his replies using the expressions in the box. Use each expression twice.

I don't know	I can't remember	I have no idea	I'm not sure

1. *I don't know if you can download songs from this website.* _____
2. _____
3. _____
4. _____
5. _____
6. _____
7. _____
8. _____

1 You should put it down.

Grammar and vocabulary | Complete the sentences with the phrasal verbs in the box. Add the correct pronouns.

look up	put away	put on	take apart	throw away
print out	✓ put down	set up	take off	turn off

1. Thanks for bringing in the box of groceries. Could you _put it down_ over here?
2. I did something awful to my computer. I tried to _____ , and now I can't get all the pieces back in it.
3. I hate those sticky price labels on things you buy. I can never _____ .
4. My game controller doesn't work anymore. I wonder if I should just _____ .
5. There's nothing good on TV. Do you mind if I _____ ?
6. I just bought these new headphones. Do you want to _____ and try them out?
7. I downloaded a video-chat app, but I can't _____ .
8. I don't know what this word means. Maybe I should _____ on the Internet.
9. My brother leaves his video games all over the floor. He should _____ , or they'll get damaged.
10. After you write documents, do you _____ to read them?

2 Step-by-step

Grammar and vocabulary | Complete the conversation with the words in the box.

hook up / the computer	✓ turn down / the air conditioning
pick up / the monitor	turn on / the radio
plug in / all the cables	turn up / the volume

Ruth We found this great apartment, but it's so cold in here.

Kate Oh, I'll _turn down the air conditioning_ .
There we go. So, what do you want to do first?

Ruth Let's put some music on.
Can you _____ ?

Kate Sure. Is that loud enough?

Ruth Not really. Can you _____ ? Thanks.

Kate I'd like to _____ , so I can check my email.

Ruth OK, let's put the computer over by the window.
I'll _____ .
You get the computer and the cables.

Kate OK. You know, I have no idea where to _____ .

Ruth I'm sure we can figure it out. Do you know where the manual is?

3 What to do?

Grammar and vocabulary

Complete the conversations using the given words. Write A's suggestions in two different ways. Then use the correct pronoun in B's response.

1. A Before you go out, _put on your hat and gloves_ .

   Before you go out, _put your hat and gloves on_ .
   (put on / your hat and gloves)

   B If I get too warm, can I _take them off_ ?
   (take off)

2. A _____ in a dictionary.

   _____ in a dictionary.
   (look up / the new words)

   B Can we _____ on the Internet?
   (look up)

3. A You have to _____ gently.

   You have to _____ gently.
   (put in / the DVD)

   B If it doesn't work, should I _____ ?
   (take out)

4. A The kitchen's so messy. We should _____ .

   The kitchen's so messy. We should _____ .
   (put away / the dishes)

   B Actually, why don't we _____ ?
   (throw away)

4 About you

Grammar

Complete the questions. Then fill in the survey with true answers.

	Yes	No
1. Can you explain to someone _how to set up voice mail on a phone_ ? (how / set up voice mail on a phone)	☐	☐
2. Do you have any idea _____ on your computer? (where / plug in the headphones)	☐	☐
3. Could you tell someone _____ ? (how / use your TV remote)	☐	☐
4. Do you know _____ on the Internet? (how / look up information)	☐	☐
5. Do you have any idea _____ when your computer crashes? (what / do)	☐	☐
6. Do you know _____ on your computer? (how / change the password)	☐	☐

Lesson C — On the other hand, . . .

1 Don't you think . . . ?

Conversation
strategies

A Match Cameron's opinions with her friends' responses.

1. I think kids watch too much TV. _f_

2. I think video games are totally boring and stupid. _____

3. I don't think people should drive big cars. _____

4. It's a shame no one writes letters anymore. I used to love getting them. _____

5. Kids need to spend less time on the computer. _____

6. I don't like shopping on the Internet. You can't see what you're buying. _____

a. I know what you mean, but with email, you can get in touch with people more often and faster.

b. I'm not so sure. Don't you think they can learn a lot online, too? I mean, there are some good educational websites.

c. Maybe. People with large families need to have big cars, though.

d. I don't know. I find it saves me time because I don't have to go to the store and wait in line.

e. I know what you mean, but there are so many different kinds of games. You could probably find something you liked.

f. That's true. On the other hand, kids need to relax sometimes, and we all have our favorite shows.

B Write your own responses to Cameron's opinions in part A. Use the expressions in the box if you disagree with her.

I know what you mean, but . . .	I don't know.
I'm not (so) sure. Don't you think . . . ?	✓ That's true. . . . , though.
Maybe.	On the other hand, . . .

1. _That's true. I think some TV shows are educational, though._

2. _____

3. _____

4. _____

5. _____

6. _____

70

2 What's your opinion?

Conversation strategies

Write opinions about the topics. Then add an expression from the box to get someone to agree with you. Use each expression twice.

| You know what I mean? | You know? | You know what I'm saying? |

1. Texting is _really convenient. But it's really annoying when you're trying to have a_ _conversation with someone who's texting at the same time. You know what I mean?_

2. Video calling is _____

3. Blogging is _____

4. Online video clips are _____

5. Tablets are _____

6. Social networking is _____

3 I don't know.

Conversation strategies

Respond to each statement with a different opinion. Try to convince the other person to agree with you.

1. Kids spend too much time on the Internet.

   I don't know. I think it's great they learn how to use computers _when they're so young. You know?_

2. Teens shouldn't go to school and work at the same time. It's too hard.

3. I think too many people are addicted to their computers and phones and everything.

4. You never know if things you see on the Internet are true.

71

1 Spam-a-lot

Reading | **A** Read the article. Then check (✓) the best title.

☐ How to Be a Successful Spammer   ☐ How Companies Avoid Spam
☐ Where to Send Spam   ☐ Don't Be a Victim – How You Can Avoid Spam

Are you fed up with junk email and spam that fills up your inbox every day? Spam isn't just annoying for home users of computers. It's becoming a serious problem for businesses, too. Getting rid of spam wastes employees' time. Spam takes up space on computers, and it can slow down – or even jam – normal email traffic.

Most people don't know how spammers get their email address, but in fact, it's very easy. Your email address may be on any number of Internet sites such as blogs, email newsletters, company directories, and many other lists on the Web. You can also become a spam victim if you've entered an online contest or responded to a survey using your email address.

Spammers also use software that generates email addresses automatically. This software makes up millions of email addresses by using common names and the addresses of well-known companies and Internet service providers. It then sends out messages to all the addresses it creates. Although some of them might not work and the messages "bounce back," many others will get through to real people. The spammers now have a valuable list of valid addresses, which they can sell to other spammers at high prices.

HOW TO PROTECT YOURSELF FROM SPAM

DO:

▶ Change your email address regularly. Create an address that is difficult to guess. For example, if your name is Kevin Smith and you love cycling, try an address like KSmith4biking@cup.org. Or if you live in Toronto, you could use KS_in_Toronto@cup.org.

▶ Have two email addresses – one for public use and a private one only for friends and family.

▶ Buy anti-spam software or use email filters. Many email programs have filters that automatically send spam to a junk-mail folder. Be sure to check the junk-mail folder periodically for any personal mail that goes there by mistake.

▶ Pay attention to typos and misspellings in email subject lines. These are warning signs of possible spam.

DON'T:

▶ Respond to spam – ever. When you respond, you confirm that your address is valid.

▶ Buy anything from a company that sent you spam. This supports their belief that spamming makes money.

B Find the underlined words in the article. Then circle the best meaning.

1. Spam can <u>jam</u> normal email traffic.   a. slow down   (b.) stop or block

2. You can become a <u>spam victim</u>.   a. someone who gets spam   b. someone who sends spam

3. The software <u>generates</u> addresses.   a. creates   b. gets rid of

4. Some messages "<u>bounce back</u>."   a. get to the people   b. go back to the spammers

5. They have a list of <u>valid</u> addresses.   a. real   b. false

6. Never <u>confirm</u> your address.   a. forget   b. say it's correct

2 Get rid of it!

Writing **A** Read the list of ideas, and add an idea of your own. Then use the ideas to complete the article.

Ways to prevent spam

- Get another email address. Use one email address for chat rooms and message boards.
- Tell friends and family how to prevent spam.
- Use spam-filtering software.
- Don't respond to spam.
- _____
  _____
  _____

How to get rid of spam

First of all, keep your personal email address private. If you want to participate in chat rooms or on _message boards_ , get a second _____ from a free email provider. Second, don't _____ to spam, even when it provides a link to "unsubscribe" from the list. Spammers see that your address is valid and sell it to other spammers. Third, use the _____ on your computer. Fourth, _____ .

Finally, tell _____ about these tips. If fewer people respond to spam, there will be less spam!

B Brainstorm ideas on one of these topics. Then plan and write a short article.

- How to avoid identity theft
- How to protect yourself from theft
- How to use the Internet safely
- How to get help with computer problems

Ideas

Unit 9 Progress chart

What can you do? Mark the boxes. ✔ = I can . . . ? = I need to review how to . . .	To review, go back to these pages in the Student's Book.
Grammar	
☐ use questions within questions and statements.	86 and 87
☐ use *how to*, *where to*, and *what to* + verb.	88
☐ use separable phrasal verbs like *turn on* and *plug in*.	88
Vocabulary	
☐ use at least 12 phrasal verbs.	88 and 89
Conversation strategies	
☐ use expressions to give a different opinion.	90
☐ use expressions to get someone to agree with me.	91
Writing	
☐ brainstorm and organize ideas to plan an article.	93

1 What have they been doing?

Grammar **A** What have these people been doing? What have they done? Complete the sentences using the present perfect continuous and then the present perfect.

1. Kazuo _'s been doing yard work_ (do yard work). He _'s planted_ (plant) some flowers.

2. Sienna and Lynn _____ (shop). They _____ (spend) over $500 each!

3. Lola _____ (run). She _____ just _____ (finish) a marathon.

4. Carmen _____ (cook) dinner. She _____ (grill) some fish.

5. Sal and Elena _____ (ski). They _____ (have) one lesson.

6. Tony _____ (do) laundry all morning. He _____ (wash) three loads.

B Circle the correct word to complete each sentence.

1. Kazuo's been doing yard work **since** / **for** a few hours.

2. Sienna and Lynn haven't shopped online **since** / **in** months.

3. Lola's been running **since** / **for** she was in college.

4. Carmen hasn't made unhealthy food **since** / **in** a long time.

5. Sal and Elena have been skiing **since** / **for** this morning.

6. Tony's been doing the laundry **for** / **in** over two hours.

2 Questions, questions . . .

Grammar Read each situation. Then use the words to write questions and answers in the present perfect continuous or the present perfect.

1. You have a friend who has been taking Spanish lessons. You ask:

   A (how long / study / Spanish) _How long have you been studying Spanish?_

   B (seven months) _I've been studying Spanish for seven months._

   A (how many words / learn) _____

   B (about 250) _____

2. You meet a famous baseball player. You ask:

   A (how long / play / baseball) _____

   B (18 years) _____

   A (how many games / win this season) _____

   B (12 out of 15) _____

3 About you

Grammar **A** Complete the questions. Use the present perfect continuous or the present perfect.

1. What _____have_____ you _been doing_____ (do) lately after class?

2. How many times _____ you _____ (go) to the movies this month?

3. Who _____ you _____ (hang out) with recently?

4. How many times _____ you _____ (eat out) at a restaurant this week?

5. _____ you _____ (study) a lot lately?

6. How many phone calls _____ you _____ (make) this week?

7. How many times _____ you _____ (oversleep) in the last month?

8. What _____ you _____ (think) about for the last hour?

9. How many books _____ you _____ (read) this year?

10. _____ you _____ (exercise) lately?

B Answer the questions in part A with true information.

1. _I've been taking guitar lessons._

2. _____

3. _____

4. _____

5. _____

6. _____

7. _____

8. _____

9. _____

10. _____

1 Crossword puzzle

Vocabulary | Complete the crossword puzzle.

Across

2. A movie with an exciting story and lots of suspense is a ___thriller___ .

3. A _____ movie is about soldiers.

5. In a romantic _____ , two people fall in love and funny things happen.

7. A movie about a real event is called a _____ story.

9. A movie that makes you cry is called a tear_____ .

10. An _____ movie has a fast-moving story and is often violent.

Down

1. A _____ -fiction movie often takes place in the future.

4. A movie with cartoon characters is an _____ movie.

6. A movie that has singing and dancing is a _____ .

8. _____ movies are often scary and have monsters in them.

2 Best of Bollywood

Vocabulary | Complete Daria's blog with the words in the box.

✓comedies endings love story set in subtitled
costumes hilarious play stunts take place

Daria's Blog

Daria 12:31 p.m.

Some of my favorite movies are musicals from Bollywood, especially the romantic _comedies_ . The movies are usually _____ _____ India, and the actors often _____ characters who fall in love. I really enjoy a good _____ _____ . They can sometimes be tearjerkers, but the nice thing about Bollywood movies is that they often have happy _____ , so you leave the movie theater feeling good. Some of them are also very funny – the last one I saw was just _____ . Some of them are historical and _____ _____ in the past. These are my favorites because the colors and the _____ are wonderful. The movies aren't usually in English, but they're _____ , so you can read while you're watching. Sometimes the movies even have fight scenes with lots of special effects and _____ . They're really great!

3 About you

Vocabulary | Write reviews of movies you've seen. Complete each sentence with the title of a movie. Then write more about each one by answering the questions.

CHOOSE A MOVIE	What type of movie is it? What's it about? Who's in it? Did you like it? Why? Why not?
1. I really enjoyed _____ _____Les Misérables_____ .	It's a musical, and it's set in France in the 1800s. Hugh Jackman plays a man who escapes from prison. Russell Crowe is the police officer who chases him. I really enjoyed the movie. It has wonderful music, and the costumes are amazing.
2. _____ _____ is playing right now.	
3. The best movie I've ever seen is _____ _____ .	
4. I didn't like _____ _____ .	

4 I still haven't see it.

Grammar and vocabulary | Complete the conversation with *already*, *still*, or *yet*.

Ann There are so many movies that I ____*still*____ haven't seen. Do you want to go see one tonight?

Gus Yeah, OK. Let's see. How about Brad Pitt's new movie? I haven't seen that _____.

Ann Oh, I've _____ seen that one. It was good. How about the new horror movie that's out? Have you seen that _____ ?

Gus No, I don't like scary movies. I'm 25, and I _____ haven't seen a horror movie.

Ann Well, there's a new animated movie out. I haven't seen that one _____ , either.

Gus Oh, great. Let's go. I've been dying to see it!

1 Favors

Conversation strategies | Complete the conversations with the expressions in the box.

I wanted to	I was wondering,
✓ I was wondering if I could	Would it be all right if I
I was wondering if you could	Would it be OK

1. **Victor** Hi, Raoul. What can I do for you?

   Raoul _I was wondering if I could_ talk to you for a moment. Is now OK?

   Victor No problem. Come on in.

   Raoul Thanks. _____ worked from home tomorrow?

   Victor Tomorrow?

   Raoul Yes. Someone is coming to fix my stove, and I need to be home to let him in. _____ with you?

   Victor Yeah, sure. I don't see why not.

   Raoul Thanks, Victor. I really appreciate it.

2. **Dad** Hi, Josie. What's up?

   Josie Hey, Dad. _____ ask you a favor.

   Dad Sure, what is it?

   Josie Well, _____ lend me some money – if that's OK.

   Dad Hmm. It depends. How much? And for what?

   Josie Well, I was thinking, your birthday is next week, right?

   Dad Yes, it is.

   Josie So, _____ could I borrow $50 to buy you your present?

2 Can I borrow the car?

Conversation strategies Stephanie's friend Ally is coming for a visit. Stephanie needs to ask her roommate Jenny for some favors. Look at her list, and complete each of her requests.

Things I need to do:

1. Ask Jenny if Ally can stay here.
2. Pick up Ally at airport – borrow Jenny's car.
3. See if Jenny wants to go sightseeing with us Saturday.
4. Organize a party Saturday night – check with Jenny.
5. Check Ally's return flight online – use Jenny's computer.

1. I wanted to _ask you if Ally could stay here_ .

2. I was wondering if I could _____ .

3. I was wondering, _____ ?

4. Would it be all right _____ ?

5. Would it be OK with you if I _____ ?

3 All right. What time?

Conversation strategies Choose the best sentence to continue each conversation. Then write *A* if the speaker is agreeing, *M* if the speaker is moving the conversation along, or *U* to show the speaker understands.

1. A I'm going grocery shopping later, and I was wondering if you could come and help me.

   B ☑ All right. What time?

   ☐ That's OK.

   `A`

2. A Do you have time to talk now?

   B Sure. Let me just put these papers away.

   ☐ Um, OK, I guess so.

   ☐ All right. What did you want to talk about?

3. A This pasta is delicious! Could you give me the recipe?

   B ☐ Sure. It's very easy.

   ☐ That would be OK.

4. A Can you help me with something?

   B ☐ OK. What do you need?

   ☐ That's all right.

5. A I'm leaving early today.

   B ☐ Right. I remember you have an appointment.

   ☐ OK. I think so, too.

79

1 Weekend favorites

Reading **A** Read the reviews. What things are reviewed? Check (✓) the boxes.

☐ a book   ☐ a movie   ☐ a phone app   ☐ a video game   ☐ a Web app

---

Weekend Blog ▭ ☐ ✕

THINGS TO KEEP YOU BUSY ON WEEKENDS

1. MOVIE EFFECTIVE

With Movie Effective, you can add special effects to your videos. Simply record a video with your smartphone camera. Then add exciting effects — just like they do in the movies. The app comes with two effects — lightning and slow motion — but you can also buy others, like sound effects. Even though I don't usually shoot or share videos personally, I found this to be a lot of fun. So, be careful — it's addictive, and you may get totally hooked!

2. ACCUSED

I really enjoyed playing this game. It combines a science-fiction setting with great action. You are a character who is wrongly accused of a crime. You have to find out who the real criminal is and get justice. Your choices determine the storyline. The action is fast-moving and there are some sad moments, so if you're very sensitive, this may not be the video game for you. However, the amazing setting and the ability to create your own story make this a great game for most players.

3. RECORDYOURRUN

If you are serious about running, hiking, biking, or even skiing, and have been wondering how to keep track of your progress, this phone app is the answer. It records your pace, distance, and time, and you can save your results and compare different exercise sessions. You can set goals for each time you go out and share your progress with friends. There's also a feature that lets your friends and family follow your progress in a race on a map. This app is the perfect way to mix technology and exercise.

4. FRETENDS

FretEnds has a fabulous Web app that will teach you how to play the guitar. You can choose to play a real guitar or a virtual one. There are eight levels of play. If you start at the beginner level, you will learn to play "Brown Eyed Girl." You need to let the app access the microphone on your computer, so it can "hear" you play. Each song is broken down into small parts. After you've learned one part, you can move on. This app is great for everyone, whether you've never played or even if you've been playing for years.

B Read the article again. Write *T* (true) or *F* (false) for each sentence. Then correct the false sentences.

1. Movie Effective helps you record videos on your smartphone. __*F*__

2. The special effects on Movie Effective are all free. _____

3. *Accused* is a romantic comedy. _____

4. *Accused* is suitable for everyone. _____

5. RecordYourRun is for people who take exercise seriously. _____

6. With RecordYourRun, people can see if their friends are winning a race. _____

7. You need to buy a guitar before you can use the FretEnds app. _____

8. The FretEnds app is not for experienced players. _____

2 Music review

Writing **A** Read the music review. Complete the sentences with *although*, *even though*, or *even if* to contrast ideas. Sometimes more than one answer is possible.

_____ *Come Away With Me* was amazingly successful and really introduced Norah Jones to the world, *Little Broken Hearts* is a much better album. Most of her earlier work uses a lot of piano, but this album focuses more on the guitar, so the sound is different. _____ most of these songs are about heartbreak, the music is beautiful and sweet. _____ you don't like sad romantic songs, you will find something to enjoy in this new collection.

– *Music Scene* magazine

B Write a review of a movie, an album, or a TV show. Use *although*, *even though*, and *even if* to contrast ideas.

Unit 10 Progress chart

What can you do? Mark the boxes. ✓ = I can . . . ? = I need to review how to . . .	To review, go back to these pages in the Student's Book.
Grammar use the present perfect and present perfect continuous.	98 and 99
use *since*, *for*, and *in* with the present perfect to show duration.	99
use *already*, *still*, and *yet* with the present perfect.	101
Vocabulary name at least 6 different kinds of movies.	100 and 101
talk about movies using at least 15 new words and expressions.	100 and 101
Conversation strategies ask for a favor politely.	102
use *All right*, *OK*, and *Sure* to agree to requests; *All right*, *OK*, and *So* to move a conversation to a new phase or topic; and *Right* to show I agree or understand.	103
Writing use *although*, *even though*, and *even if* to contrast ideas.	105

1 It could be . . .

Grammar | Complete the sentences with the expressions in the box. Then write a second sentence using the cues and an appropriate modal.

can't be the winners	may be taking a driving test	✓ must be learning to drive
could be taking a hard test	might be the best student	must be the winners

1. He _must be learning to drive_.
   It could / might / may be his first lesson.
   (It / be / his first lesson)

2. He _____.
   _____.
   (It / be / his first lesson)

3. She _____.
   _____.
   (She / feel proud)

4. She _____.
   _____.
   (She / be nervous)

5. They _____.
   _____.
   (They / practice a lot)

6. They _____.
   _____.
   (They / be disappointed)

2 He must be crazy!

Grammar | Circle the correct words to complete the sentences.

1. **Mandy** What's he doing? He (**must be**) / **can't be** crazy!

   Molly He **might be** / **can't be** an acrobat with the circus.

   Mandy You're right. He **must practice** / **must be practicing** for tonight's show.

   Molly That's amazing! I mean, it **can't be** / **might be** easy to bend like that.

   Mandy Yeah, it **could be** / **must not be** painful, too.

   Molly Well, I certainly won't try that!

2. **Jason** How old is that kid? She **must be** / **can't be** more than five years old.

   Peter Yeah, you're right. She **must not be** / **might be** about four or five.

   Jason She's really good. She **must play** / **must be playing** every day for hours and hours.

   Peter She makes it look so easy, too. I wonder what her parents think. They **could be** / **must be** so proud.

   Jason Yeah, she **could be** / **can't be** the youngest professional piano player in the world.

3 About you

Grammar | Think of someone you know who is not in the room with you now. Answer the questions about him or her using *must*, *may*, *might*, *could*, or *can't*.

1. Where do you think he or she is right now?

   It's Saturday afternoon, so he might be on the golf course. He can't be at work.

2. What do you think he or she is doing?

   _____

3. How do you think he or she is feeling?

   _____

4. What do you think he or she is wearing?

   _____

5. Who do you think he or she is with?

   _____

6. What do you think he or she is thinking about right now?

   _____

Ups and downs

1 Scrambled up

Grammar and vocabulary

A Write the adjective for each definition. You can check your answers in a dictionary. Then use the letters in the boxes to answer the question below.

1. Greatly surprised   <u>a</u> <u>m</u> [<u>a</u>] <u>z</u> <u>e</u> <u>d</u>

2. Upset or not pleased   __ __ [ ] __ __ __

3. Makes you feel excited   __ [ ] __ __ __ __ __ __

4. Irritating   __ __ __ __ __ __ [ ] __ __

5. Not interesting   __ [ ] __ __ __

6. Not expected or normal   __ __ [ ] __ __ __ __ __ __ __ __ __

7. Frightening   [ ] __ __ __ __

How might you feel the first time you try something new? <u>a</u> __ __ __ __ __ __

B Complete the sentences with the other forms of the adjectives in part A.

1. Someone who upsets you or makes you slightly angry is _____<u>annoying</u>_____ .

2. If someone gives you a present for no reason, you might be _____ .

3. If you have nothing to do, you might feel _____ .

4. When you're very afraid of something, you might feel _____ .

5. Someone who learns to speak six or seven languages is truly _____ .

6. When you're going to do something fun, you are —————— about it.

7. When you can't remember a word in English, you probably feel _____ .

2 Good news, bad news

Grammar
and
vocabulary

Complete the emails. Use the correct forms of the adjectives.

New Message

To: EmmaP@cup.com
From: shak91@cup.com
Subject: **My short story**

Hey Emma,

I'm so __*excited*__ (excite). Remember the short story I wrote for English class last month? Well, my teacher sent it to a competition, and guess what? It won first prize! The judges said my story was very _____ (interest). I knew my teacher was _____ (please) with my work. She said my story was _____ (fascinate). But I never thought she would enter it in a competition! I was totally _____ (shock) when she told me. And all my classmates were totally _____ (jealous). What's new and exciting with you?

Shakira

New Message

To: shak91@cup.com
From: EmmaP@cup.com
Subject: **My short story**

Hi Shakira,

Congratulations! I wish I had _____ (excite) news for you, too, but I don't. Unfortunately, I failed my driver's test last week. I was really _____ (disappoint). It's just so _____ (embarrass) – it's the third time I've failed the test. The driving instructor told me to make a right-hand turn, and I turned left instead. I guess I got a little _____ (confuse). I could tell the instructor was really _____ (annoy) with me! My dad told me not to get _____ (frustrate). He said he failed his driver's test five times before he finally passed, but I'm starting to get _____ (worry). Well, talk to you later.

Emma

---

3 About you

Grammar
and
vocabulary

How would you feel in these situations? Complete the sentences with true information.

1. You fail a test that you have studied very hard for.
   I would feel __*disappointed if I failed a test that I thought I was prepared for*__ .
   It might be __*embarrassing if my friends found out*__ .

2. Your friend doesn't show up for a date.
   I would get _____ .
   I might feel _____ .

3. You are home alone during a storm.
   I might feel _____ .
   It could be _____ .

4. Someone is telling you a story you've already heard ten times.
   I might feel _____ .
   I would probably think _____ .

1 You must be excited.

Complete the responses in the conversations to show understanding. Use *must be* and an adjective.

1. I'm learning how to design a website. | *That must be hard* _____ .

2. My brother always takes my stuff. | That _____ .

3. I lost my wallet and credit cards at the mall. | You _____ .

4. I'm going to climb Mount Rainier next month. | You _____ .

5. I didn't win the poetry contest. | You _____ .

6. My ex-boyfriend is dating my best friend. | That _____ .

2 Explanations

Complete the conversation with *you see* or *I see*, or leave a blank where neither one is appropriate.

Walt Hi, Reg. I'm sorry I'm late. I didn't hear my alarm.
_You see_____ , I was working on my report until
about 3:30 this morning.

Reg Uh-huh, _____ . So, will it be ready for
the meeting with the boss?

Walt _____ Yes. I just have to make some copies.
What time is the meeting?

Reg Well, it was at 11:00, but the boss called me about
half an hour ago, and it's now at 2:30. She's meeting
someone for lunch, _____ , and she has
to leave at 11:30.

Walt Oh, _____ . So, I guess I didn't have to rush.

Reg Well, at least it's all done now, and you can relax.

3 An author in Paris

Complete the conversation with the expressions in the box. Use each expression twice.

I see	that must be	you must be	you see

Akina   Hey, Omar. I hear you're going away for a while. Where to?

Omar   Yeah, I'm leaving for Paris next week.

Akina   You're kidding! Wow, _you must be_ excited!

Omar   I am. I've never been there before. _____ , I'm going to do some research
for my next book. That's always the best part – the research.

Akina   I bet. _____ fun. So, what's your book about?

Omar   It's a love story, of course.

Akina   _____ . Uh . . . can you share any details yet?

Omar   I guess. Hmm . . . let's see. It's about a young girl who goes to visit a friend in Paris.
And well, you know, she meets a mysterious young man, they fall in love, and lots
of things happen.

Akina   Really? What kind of things?

Omar   Well, I don't want to say yet. _____ , I want to keep the details a surprise.

Akina   I understand. But, gosh, _____ hard. I can never keep secrets.

Omar   I know what you mean. It's difficult sometimes.

Akina   So, tell me what else you're doing in Paris.

Omar   Oh. I'm going to read from my last novel at an English-language bookstore.

Akina   Great! _____ pleased about that. Will you be nervous?

Omar   No, not at all. I've done it several times. It's part of the job of being a writer.

Akina   _____ . Well, have a wonderful trip. Good luck with your research.

Omar   Thanks. I'll tell you all about it when I get back.

1 Child prodigies

Reading | **A Read the article. What does "child prodigy" mean?**

☐ someone under the age of 15 ☐ a child with a special talent ☐ a child who is famous

CHILD PRODIGIES:

Nature OR Nurture?

Mozart wrote his first minuet at age six. Cellist Yo-Yo Ma first performed in public at the age of five. William James Sidis read Homer in Greek at age four and was the youngest person ever to attend Harvard University at 11. Ukrainian chess player Sergey Karjakin became the youngest international grand master at 12. Pablo Picasso first publicly exhibited his paintings at age 13.

Many parents may hope for a genius child, but there can be a price to pay. Some child prodigies never experience a normal childhood, often because it's difficult for them to make friends, and they suffer socially. Some genius children even have mental breakdowns at an early age, and gifted child athletes or musicians can be permanently injured from practicing too hard.

We often hear stories of parents who push their children too hard. However, some experts say that for the most part, "pushy parent" is an unfair label: Parents don't push prodigies, prodigies push parents. Many gifted children quickly become bored with school and homework that is too easy. For these kids, school is frustrating, and they risk losing interest in it altogether. It's better to allow these children to skip grades, experts say, than to let them become disappointed in school.

Are prodigies born, or are they created? The short answer is: we don't know. Certainly, many parents of gifted children provide a stimulating environment: They read to their children at an early age, take them to museums and concerts, and give them a lot of independence. But experts advise parents not to be disappointed if their child isn't an early genius. Mozart was a child prodigy; Einstein was not. But the world is still amazed by them both.

B Find a word or expression in the article for each meaning below.

1. go to, or be present at (a place or an event) (paragraph 1) __*attend*__
2. psychological problems (paragraph 2) _____
3. talented; exceptional (paragraph 3) _____
4. interesting; encouraging you to learn (paragraph 4) _____

C Read the article again. Then answer the questions.

1. Who's the youngest prodigy mentioned in the article?

   _____

2. What are three disadvantages of being a child prodigy?

   _____

3. What problems do some gifted children have with school?

   _____

4. How do some parents help their gifted children develop?

   _____

2 My child is a prodigy!

Writing | **A**   Read the letter from a parent to a school principal. Circle the expressions that give impressions or opinions. Underline the statements that are stated as fact.

=== 𝑀𝑇 ===

Dear Dr. Evans,

My child is enrolled in your school. (I believe that) he is a very gifted student, and I feel that he is bored in his classes. It seems to me that he is becoming increasingly frustrated and anxious because he has lost interest in school. Last year he was the top student in his class, but this year his grades are slipping. My impression is that he needs to take more difficult classes. In my opinion, he is not finding his current classes challenging enough. Can you help?

Sincerely,

Marsha Taylor

B   Write a letter to the editor of a local newspaper about one of the topics below or your own idea. Use the expressions from part A.

- There aren't enough leisure facilities for local teens.
- We need healthier food options in schools.
- There's too much litter on city streets.

Unit 11 Progress chart

What can you do? Mark the boxes. ✔ = I can . . . ? = I need to review how to . . .	To review, go back to these pages in the Student's Book.
Grammar — use the modals *must*, *may*, *might*, *can't*, and *could* to speculate.	108 and 109
use adjectives ending in *-ed* to describe how someone feels.	110 and 111
use adjectives ending in *-ing* to describe someone or something.	110 and 111
Vocabulary — name at least 12 adjectives to describe feelings and reactions.	110 and 111
Conversation strategies — use *That must be* or *You must be* + adjective to show I understand.	112
use *You see* to explain something and *I see* to show I understand.	113
Writing — use expressions like *I feel* to give impressions or opinions.	115

1 And now, the news . . .

Grammar | **Complete the news reports. Use the simple past passive.**

1. Newtown Park train station __was closed__
   (close) this morning after a bag _____
   (find) on a train. Several trains _____
   (delay), and some _____ (cancel). The
   bag _____ (remove) from the station
   and _____ (search). Police said later
   that the bag was full of clothes. The train station
   _____ (reopen) after two hours.

2. A woman _____ (rescue) earlier today
   after she climbed onto her roof to repair her
   chimney. Firefighters _____ (call) to the
   scene after neighbors heard the woman shout
   for help. Fortunately, the woman _____
   (not hurt), but she _____ (take) to the
   local hospital and _____ (release) later
   this afternoon.

3. The National Museum _____ (break into)
   last night, and three valuable paintings
   _____ (steal). The area around the
   museum _____ (close off) following the
   incident, and bystanders _____
   (interview). Police are now looking for two young
   men who _____ (see) nearby.

2 More news

Grammar | **Rewrite the sentences using the simple past passive.**

1. They delayed the game for two hours.   *The game was delayed for two hours.*
2. Someone stole a ring from an exhibit.   _____
3. They canceled the rock concert.   _____
4. A woman found a wallet on a bus.   _____
5. They took two people to the hospital.   _____
6. Someone rescued a man from a fire.   _____

3 What happened?

Grammar | **Look at the picture. What do you think happened? Write a news report. Use the verbs in the box or your own ideas. Use the simple past passive. Be creative with your facts!**

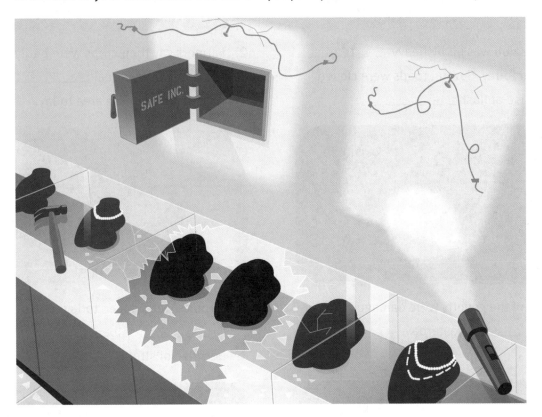

break into
close
find
hurt
open
rob
steal
take

News Report: Stolen Goods!
A downtown jewelry store was robbed yesterday.
_____
_____
_____
_____
_____
_____

1 All kinds of weather

Vocabulary | Look at the pictures. Complete the sentences with the words in the box.

aftershocks	floods	hurricane	✓rains	tornado
earthquake	hailstorm	lightning	thunderstorm	winds

1. The region was hit by heavy ____*rains*____ earlier today. Several roads were closed because of flash _____ .

2. Farmers say their crops were badly damaged by the ice from a freak _____ that passed through the area today.

3. Parts of the country were damaged by a _____ yesterday.

4. Airports were closed today due to _____ Albert. Flights were canceled because of strong _____ and rain.

5. The area was hit yesterday by a major _____ , measuring 5.6 on the Richter scale. _____ were felt throughout the area.

6. Electricity throughout the city was disrupted by thunder and _____ from a severe _____ .

2 What was the cause?

Grammar and vocabulary | Look at each pair of pictures. What caused the damage? Write a sentence using the given word and *by*.

start

blow down

strike

cause

crack

1. _A fire was started by a candle._

2. _____

3. _____

4. _____

5. _____

3 In the news

Grammar | Rewrite the sentences using the simple past passive and the adverb given.

1. The fire damaged the building. (partially)
   The building was partially damaged by the fire.

2. The storm disrupted train services. (temporarily)
   _____

3. Flash floods damaged several houses in the area. (badly)
   _____

4. A wildfire injured three firefighters. (seriously)
   _____

5. A tornado destroyed a small farm. (completely)
   _____

Did you hear about . . . ?

1 News travels fast!

Complete the conversation with the expressions in the box. Use each expression only once.

did I tell you	guess what	you know
did you hear about ✓have you heard		you know what

Don   _Have you heard_   the news about Henry?

Nadia   No. What happened to him?

Don   Well, _____ he goes mountain biking, right?

Nadia   Yes. I've seen him on his bike a lot.

Don   Well, he went out biking yesterday, and _____ ? He was in the mountains during that big thunderstorm in the afternoon. He had to sit under a tree to avoid the lightning. . . .

Nadia   Under a tree? _____ ? That's really dangerous.

Don   It is?

Nadia   Oh, yeah. _____ those golfers who were hit by lightning under a tree?

Don   No. Oh, that's awful.

Nadia   Yeah. They were taken to the hospital and everything. But amazingly, they were OK.

Don   That was lucky. By the way, _____ about my car? The roof was damaged in that storm, too. It was hit by the hailstones.

2 About you

Write sentences introducing some news. Use true information.

1. _You know my friend Callie? She got a new laptop for her birthday._
   (good news about a friend)

2. _____
   (fun news about yourself)

3. _____
   (bad news about a local sports team)

4. _____
   (news about the local weather)

5. _____
   (interesting news about your favorite actor or singer)

6. _____
   (news about a family member)

7. _____
   (news about another city)

3 The funny thing was . . .

Conversation strategies | Circle the best way to complete each sentence.

1. I lost my bag last week, and then I found it outside my dorm room. The funny thing was, **everything was stolen** /(**nothing was stolen**).

2. Thieves broke into my car last week, and the worst thing was, **they took my favorite bag** / **the inside of the car was completely cleaned**.

3. Some neighbors of ours got married last month, and the weird thing is, **they didn't tell anyone about it** / **we all had a great time**.

4. We had a great weekend at the beach. The best thing was, **the water was so warm** / **it rained**.

5. That movie was incredible. The only thing was, **the ending was the best** / **the ending was disappointing**.

6. We went out for dinner last night, and the food was terrible. The other thing was, **the waiters were helpful** / **it was really expensive**.

4 The whole story

Conversation strategies | Complete the conversations with the expressions in the box.

Did I tell you?	The best thing is,
✓ Did you hear	The funny thing is,

1. A _Did you hear_ about the new vacation schedule?

   B No, I didn't. What about it?

   A We get an extra week of vacation.

   B Great!

   A _____ the extra week is in February. That means we can plan a nice, long ski vacation!

2. A _____ There was a small fire at school yesterday.

   B Really? Where?

   A It was in the science lab. Some students were doing an experiment, and it exploded.

   B I hope no one was hurt.

   A Everyone is fine. _____ the students all got A's!

1 Only the news that interests you

Reading | **A** Read the article. Which news sources do young people use?

CHANGING SOURCES OF NEWS

Far fewer people, especially the young, get their news from traditional news sources (either print or television), according to the most recent surveys. Instead, they are getting news from online sources and social networking sites, using their cell phones, tablets, and other mobile devices. In just two years, the number of people who get news from social networks doubled, and now about a third of young readers get their news this way. Although half of all Americans still watch TV to keep up with events, only 28% of people between the ages of 18 and 29 do so.

This use of social networks for news can be seen in Europe also. One in five people in the United Kingdom, and 43% of young people, get their news from the most popular social networking and microblogging sites. According to a recent study in Spain, three-quarters of the people between the ages of 16 and 30 got their news from a social networking site, as compared to only 28% from newspapers.

The addition of these news channels may contribute to "news fatigue," or a feeling of being overloaded with news. A study that was conducted by the University of Texas found that the way we get the news affects whether we feel information overload. People who got their news from computers and tablets were much more likely to feel overloaded, while people who got their news from TV or read it on their cell phone were less likely to experience this. The study showed that reading the same news on a computer was felt to be more tiring than reading it on a phone, perhaps because options seem more limited on a phone, and so more manageable. People on computers and tablets usually see many more links than people who use phone apps.

News organizations have adapted their news presentation style to try to prevent or reduce news fatigue. Some provide news in three forms: breaking headlines, short present-tense stories, and links to longer stories. By cutting down the number of headline updates, they also hope to reduce news fatigue.

B Read the article again. Circle the best alternatives to complete the sentences.

1. The author suggests in the article that young people and older people _____ .
   a. get news the same way   b. often get their news from different sources

2. One news source that is growing in popularity is _____ .
   a. microblogging sites   b. television news

3. Three out of four young people get their news from social networks in _____ .
   a. Spain   b. the United States

4. People who get their news on computers are more likely to be overloaded than if they get their news on _____ .
   a. tablets   b. smartphones

5. One way that people get news fatigue is by reading too many _____ .
   a. headline updates   b. longer stories

2 News survey

Writing **A** Read the survey. Then complete the article below with the expressions in the box.

Barnesville News **Survey:**

1. Do you read the *Barnesville News* every day? 👍**Yes** 49% 👎**No** 51%
2. What's your favorite section?

Section		%
Weather		0%
Local	▬	9%
Sports	▬	10%
Arts	▬▬	20%
International	▬▬▬▬	59%
Travel	▌	2%

almost
✓ half
majority
none
out of
20%

About ___half___ of the people we surveyed read the *Barnesville News* every day. The _____ of *Barnesville News* readers prefer the international section. Only one _____ ten readers chose the sports section as their favorite. _____ 10% of readers enjoy the local section, while _____ of them are interested in the arts section. _____ of them chose the weather as their favorite.

B How many of your friends read a local or national news website?
Write a paragraph like the one in part A to show the statistics.

_____
_____
_____
_____
_____
_____

Unit 12 Progress chart

What can you do? Mark the boxes. ☑ = I can . . . ? = I need to review how to . . .		To review, go back to these pages in the Student's Book.
Grammar	☐ use the simple past passive to discuss the news.	118, 119, and 120
	☐ use the passive + *by* to introduce the "doer" or cause of an action.	120 and 121
Vocabulary	☐ name at least 10 types of extreme weather or natural disasters.	120 and 121
	☐ name at least 4 adverbs with the simple past passive.	120 and 121
Conversation strategies	☐ introduce news with expressions like *Guess what?*	122
	☐ use expressions like *The thing is . . .* to introduce issues.	123
Writing	☐ write about statistics.	125

Illustration credits

Photo credits

Text credits

The top 500 spoken words

This is a list of the top 500 words in spoken North American English. It is based on a sample of four and a half million words of conversation from the Cambridge International Corpus. The most frequent word, *I*, is at the top of the list.

1. I	40. really	79. see
2. and	41. with	80. how
3. the	42. he	81. they're
4. you	43. one	82. kind
5. uh	44. are	83. here
6. to	45. this	84. from
7. a	46. there	85. did
8. that	47. I'm	86. something
9. it	48. all	87. too
10. of	49. if	88. more
11. yeah	50. no	89. very
12. know	51. get	90. want
13. in	52. about	91. little
14. like	53. at	92. been
15. they	54. out	93. things
16. have	55. had	94. an
17. so	56. then	95. you're
18. was	57. because	96. said
19. but	58. go	97. there's
20. is	59. up	98. I've
21. it's	60. she	99. much
22. we	61. when	100. where
23. huh	62. them	101. two
24. just	63. can	102. thing
25. oh	64. would	103. her
26. do	65. as	104. didn't
27. don't	66. me	105. other
28. that's	67. mean	106. say
29. well	68. some	107. back
30. for	69. good	108. could
31. what	70. got	109. their
32. on	71. OK	110. our
33. think	72. people	111. guess
34. right	73. now	112. yes
35. not	74. going	113. way
36. um	75. were	114. has
37. or	76. lot	115. down
38. my	77. your	116. we're
39. be	78. time	117. any

The top 500 spoken words

118. he's	161. five	204. sort
119. work	162. always	205. great
120. take	163. school	206. bad
121. even	164. look	207. we've
122. those	165. still	208. another
123. over	166. around	209. car
124. probably	167. anything	210. true
125. him	168. kids	211. whole
126. who	169. first	212. whatever
127. put	170. does	213. twenty
128. years	171. need	214. after
129. sure	172. us	215. ever
130. can't	173. should	216. find
131. pretty	174. talking	217. care
132. gonna	175. last	218. better
133. stuff	176. thought	219. hard
134. come	177. doesn't	220. haven't
135. these	178. different	221. trying
136. by	179. money	222. give
137. into	180. long	223. I'd
138. went	181. used	224. problem
139. make	182. getting	225. else
140. than	183. same	226. remember
141. year	184. four	227. might
142. three	185. every	228. again
143. which	186. new	229. pay
144. home	187. everything	230. try
145. will	188. many	231. place
146. nice	189. before	232. part
147. never	190. though	233. let
148. only	191. most	234. keep
149. his	192. tell	235. children
150. doing	193. being	236. anyway
151. cause	194. bit	237. came
152. off	195. house	238. six
153. I'll	196. also	239. family
154. maybe	197. use	240. wasn't
155. real	198. through	241. talk
156. why	199. feel	242. made
157. big	200. course	243. hundred
158. actually	201. what's	244. night
159. she's	202. old	245. call
160. day	203. done	246. saying

The top 500 spoken words

247. dollars
248. live
249. away
250. either
251. read
252. having
253. far
254. watch
255. week
256. mhm
257. quite
258. enough
259. next
260. couple
261. own
262. wouldn't
263. ten
264. interesting
265. am
266. sometimes
267. bye
268. seems
269. heard
270. goes
271. called
272. point
273. ago
274. while
275. fact
276. once
277. seen
278. wanted
279. isn't
280. start
281. high
282. somebody
283. let's
284. times
285. guy
286. area
287. fun
288. they've
289. you've

290. started
291. job
292. says
293. play
294. usually
295. wow
296. exactly
297. took
298. few
299. child
300. thirty
301. buy
302. person
303. working
304. half
305. looking
306. someone
307. coming
308. eight
309. love
310. everybody
311. able
312. we'll
313. life
314. may
315. both
316. type
317. end
318. least
319. told
320. saw
321. college
322. ones
323. almost
324. since
325. days
326. couldn't
327. gets
328. guys
329. god
330. country
331. wait
332. yet

333. believe
334. thinking
335. funny
336. state
337. until
338. husband
339. idea
340. name
341. seven
342. together
343. each
344. hear
345. help
346. nothing
347. parents
348. room
349. today
350. makes
351. stay
352. mom
353. sounds
354. change
355. understand
356. such
357. gone
358. system
359. comes
360. thank
361. show
362. thousand
363. left
364. friends
365. class
366. already
367. eat
368. small
369. boy
370. paper
371. world
372. best
373. water
374. myself
375. run

The top 500 spoken words

376. they'll	418. company	460. sorry
377. won't	419. friend	461. living
378. movie	420. set	462. drive
379. cool	421. minutes	463. outside
380. news	422. morning	464. bring
381. number	423. between	465. easy
382. man	424. music	466. stop
383. basically	425. close	467. percent
384. nine	426. leave	468. hand
385. enjoy	427. wife	469. gosh
386. bought	428. knew	470. top
387. whether	429. pick	471. cut
388. especially	430. important	472. computer
389. taking	431. ask	473. tried
390. sit	432. hour	474. gotten
391. book	433. deal	475. mind
392. fifty	434. mine	476. business
393. months	435. reason	477. anybody
394. women	436. credit	478. takes
395. month	437. dog	479. aren't
396. found	438. group	480. question
397. side	439. turn	481. rather
398. food	440. making	482. twelve
399. looks	441. American	483. phone
400. summer	442. weeks	484. program
401. hmm	443. certain	485. without
402. fine	444. less	486. moved
403. hey	445. must	487. gave
404. student	446. dad	488. yep
405. agree	447. during	489. case
406. mother	448. lived	490. looked
407. problems	449. forty	491. certainly
408. city	450. air	492. talked
409. second	451. government	493. beautiful
410. definitely	452. eighty	494. card
411. spend	453. wonderful	495. walk
412. happened	454. seem	496. married
413. hours	455. wrong	497. anymore
414. war	456. young	498. you'll
415. matter	457. places	499. middle
416. supposed	458. girl	500. tax
417. worked	459. happen	

TOUCHSTONE

MARCIA FISK ONG

SERIES AUTHORS

MICHAEL MCCARTHY

JEANNE MCCARTEN

HELEN SANDIFORD

VIDEO ACTIVITY PAGES

CAMBRIDGE
UNIVERSITY PRESS

Contents

Character descriptions

Touchstone Video is a fun-filled, compelling situational comedy featuring a group of young people who are friends. David Parker is a reporter. His roommate is Alex Santos, a personal trainer. David's friend Gio Ferrari is a student visiting from Italy. Liz Martin is a singer and Web designer. She lives with Yoko Suzuki, a chef. Kim Davis is David's co-worker. She works in an office.

Through the daily encounters and activities of these characters, you have the opportunity to see and hear the language of the Student's Book vividly come to life in circumstances both familiar and entertaining.

This is David Parker.
He's a reporter.

This is Yoko Suzuki.
She's a chef.

This is Alex Santos.
He's a personal trainer.

This is Gio Ferrari.
He's a student.
He's from Italy.

This is Liz Martin.
She's a Web designer
and singer.

This is Kim Davis.
She's David's co-worker.

The Video

Welcome to the *Touchstone* Video. In this video you will get to know six people who are friends: David, Liz, Yoko, Alex, Kim, and Gio. You can read about them on page iv.

You will also hear them use the English that you are studying in the *Touchstone* Student's Books. Each of the four levels of the Video breaks down as follows:

Episode 1	Act 1	*Student's Book units 1–3*
	Act 2	
	Act 3	

Episode 2	Act 1	*Student's Book units 4–6*
	Act 2	
	Act 3	

Episode 3	Act 1	*Student's Book units 7–9*
	Act 2	
	Act 3	

Episode 4	Act 1	*Student's Book units 10–12*
	Act 2	
	Act 3	

Explanation of the DVD Menu

To play one Episode of the Video:
- On the Main Menu, select *Episode Menu*.
- On the Episode Menu, select the appropriate *Play Episode*.

To play one Act of the Video:
- On the Main Menu, select *Episode Menu*.
- On the Episode Menu, select *Act Menu*.
- On the Act Menu, select the appropriate *Play Act*.

To play the Video with subtitles:
- On the Main Menu, Episode Menu, or Act Menu, select *Subtitles*.
- On the Subtitles Menu, select *Subtitles on*. The DVD will then automatically take you back to the menu you were on before.

To cancel the subtitles:
- On the Main Menu, Episode Menu, or Act Menu, select *Subtitles*.
- On the Subtitles Menu, select *Subtitles off*. The DVD will then automatically take you back to the menu you were on before.

The Worksheets

For each Act there are *Before you watch*, *While you watch*, and *After you watch* worksheets.

For *While you watch* worksheets:
- Find **DVD**[0] on your worksheet.
- Input this number on the Video menu using your remote control. The DVD will then play only the segment of the Video you need to watch to complete the task.

We hope you enjoy the *Touchstone* Video!

Episode 3 The Big Move

Act 1

Before you watch

A Read the reported speech sentences. Write the direct speech.

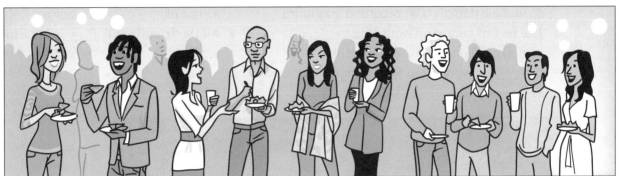

1. Emma asked how many people he had invited.
   How many people did he invite? _____

2. Paula told Emma that she would be right back.
   _____

3. Matt said that he was having a good time.
   _____

4. Scott asked Mary if she had seen any good movies recently.
   _____

5. Kathy asked Jim if he would give her a ride home later.
   _____

B Read the sentences. Choose the expression that is closest in meaning to the underlined word(s).

a. agree to do	c. busy, not available	e. throw out
b. bring success or good results	d. finish (something)	

1. Sorry, I can't see you this afternoon. I'm <u>tied up</u> in meetings until five. _____
2. OK, everyone! Let's <u>wrap</u> it <u>up</u>. Time to go home! _____
3. Starting a company is a big investment, but it often <u>pays off</u> in the end. _____
4. I cleaned out my closet last night. I'm <u>getting rid of</u> a lot of my old clothes. _____
5. I'm willing to <u>take on</u> some extra work. I really need the money. _____

C Match the sentences with the responses. Then practice with a partner.

1. Where is Sam? The meeting starts at 9:00! _____
2. Why did Kate have to leave early today? _____
3. The boss doesn't look happy today! _____
4. Why didn't Ron come to the party last week? _____
5. Rosa never e-mailed me back. _____

a. Uh-oh, something must have happened.
b. She might not have gotten the message.
c. I don't know. He might have forgotten about it.
d. She must have had an appointment.
e. I'm not sure. He may have been sick.

While you watch

A Circle the correct answers.

1. Liz and Yoko went to get _____ .
   a. coffee   b. a truck
2. Liz is moving to _____ .
   a. New York   b. Los Angeles
3. Last month, Liz _____ .
   a. made a demo   b. recorded an album
4. The record company wants Liz to _____ .
   a. make a demo   b. sing in clubs
5. Liz _____ working in Web design.
   a. has stopped   b. will continue

6. David is _____ about Liz moving.
   a. worried   b. depressed
7. Liz has more _____ than Yoko has.
   a. time   b. stuff
8. Yoko is moving _____ town.
   a. out of   b. across
9. All the friends will _____ Liz a lot.
   a. miss   b. visit

B Circle the correct words. (You may need to watch the video more than once.) Then answer the question.

1. Why does Gio think Liz and Yoko are late?
   He's pretty certain that Liz and Yoko got **tied up in traffic** / **lost**.
2. What does he say about the truck?
   He thinks the truck may not have been **running properly** / **ready**.
3. What does David say about the situation?
   He thinks it's **suprising** / **rude** that they haven't called.
4. What does Alex say?
   He thinks it's possible that they forgot their **driver's licenses** / **cell phones**.
5. Why else do you think Liz and Yoko might be late?

   _____

While you watch

DVD 34
VHS 28:06
−32:24

C Who says these things? Watch the video and check (✓) the correct names.

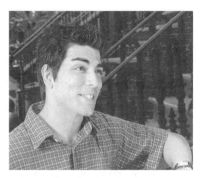

	Alex	David	Gio
1. I never get up this early.			
2. Well, moving day can be pretty crazy.			
3. How did all this happen so fast?			
4. Anyway, suddenly, the next thing I hear she's moving out there!			
5. Do you know what she's doing about her Web design business?			
6. After all, this is a once-in-a-lifetime opportunity for her.			
7. I really hope this pays off for her in the end.			
8. All of her stuff is going into storage for now.			
9. Yoko must have been kind of upset when Liz told her she was leaving.			
10. But Yoko knows it's Liz's dream to record her own album.			
11. Where's the truck?			

DVD 35
VHS 29:50
−32:03

D Check (✓) the words and expressions that are used to describe Liz.

☐ not taking on new work ☐ tough ☐ upset
☐ confident ☐ thinks before acting ☐ can't afford the apartment
☐ determined ☐ doesn't have much stuff
☐ risky ☐ keeps everything

DVD 36
VHS 29:20
−30:19

E Listen for these sentences. What does Gio say exactly? Circle the correct words.

1. *Gio* Basically, it did happen pretty fast. Liz **told** / **was telling** me that the record company called her a week after she got home. They **asked** / **were asking** her when she could come out to L.A. to record an album, and she told them that **she could** / **she'd** come right away.

2. *Gio* Yeah, and Liz **told** / **was telling** me that the company is getting her a manager and everything. **Apparently** / **Evidently**, they want her to start singing in clubs out there . . .

3. *Gio* Um, **Yoko said** / **according to Yoko**, Liz wrapped up all her projects last week. **Apparently** / **Evidently**, she's not taking on any new work for now.

4. *Gio* Uh-huh. She **told** / **was telling** me that she was determined to succeed.

After you watch

A **What can you remember? Answer the questions.**

1. What has happened to Liz recently? How is her life changing?

   _____

   _____

2. Do you agree with David that Liz is taking a big risk? What would you do in Liz's position?

   _____

   _____

B **Use the expressions in the box to report the following lines from the story. (You may or may not choose to "shift back" verb tenses.)**

> David / Gio / Alex said . . .
> David / Gio / Alex was saying . . .
> According to David / Gio / Alex . . .

1. David: "It all seems a little risky."

   David said it all seemed a little risky.

   OR _According to David, it all seems a little risky._

2. Gio: "Liz is not the impulsive type at all."

   _____

3. Alex: "Liz always thinks before she acts."

   _____

4. Gio: "All of Liz's stuff is going into storage for now."

   _____

5. Alex: "Yoko has to move across town."

   _____

C **Write some things that people have recently told you about these topics. Then choose two pieces of news and tell a partner about them. Say why this information is interesting or important to you.**

Write some news about someone's . . .

1. job: _____
2. plans: _____
3. family: _____
4. possessions: _____

"Apparently, my friend Shaun is unhappy with his job. He told me that he's looking for a new one. I'm a little worried that he won't be able to find one."

"Gina said that she was going to China this summer. I'm really excited for her."

Act 2

Before you watch

A Complete the sentences with the words in the box.

| ✓ faucet | inspect | screwdriver | security deposit | showerhead | water damage |

1. The __faucet_____ in the kitchen won't stop dripping! Can you help me fix it?
2. I just got a new dresser, and I need a _____ to put it together.
3. Before you move into your new apartment, you should _____ it carefully. You need to make sure that nothing is damaged.
4. I think our roof is leaking. There is some _____ on the ceiling.
5. *A* This new _____ is supposed to cut our water use in half.
   B But I like to take baths.
6. If I rent this apartment, I have to pay the first month's rent and a _____ .

B Match the sentences.

1. Our TV and VCR aren't working. __d__
2. My watch strap is broken. _____
3. There's a stain on the carpet. _____
4. I don't like the color of this room. _____
5. The faucet won't stop dripping. _____
6. These windows are very dirty. _____

a. They really need washing.
b. Do you think the knob needs to be replaced?
c. It really needs replacing.
d. We need to get someone to fix them.
e. Let's have someone paint it soon.
f. I'm going to have it cleaned next week.

C Use the words in parentheses to complete each sentence with a past modal.

1. I had a reservation for dinner tonight, but the restaurant said it was for next week.
   Someone __must have made_____ (must / make) a mistake.
2. I feel really bad because I yelled at my brother. I _____ (should not / get) angry at him.
3. I got a bad grade on my test. I guess I _____ (could / study) harder for it.
4. I was late for work this morning. I _____ (should / leave) home earlier.
5. Kathy said she would call me right back, but that was over an hour ago! I guess she _____ (must / forget).

While you watch

A Number the scenes in the correct order.

a. _____

b. _____

c. _____

d. _____

e. _____

f. _____

B Watch the video and number the sentences in the correct order.

_____ Maybe I can fix it.

_____ So, where do you want this?

_____ Is everything OK?

_____ There was a bit of a mix-up.

_____ I should get that fixed before the landlord comes.

_____ Ooh. What happened here?

_____ . . . why don't we help you with your boxes?

_____ I should have known that.

DVD 39
VHS 32:29
−37:12

C Circle all the correct answers. (One, two, or three answers are possible.)

1. The rental company had a reservation for the _____ .
   a. morning   b. afternoon   c. evening
2. Liz got upset because she was _____ .
   a. stressed   b. frustrated   c. tired
3. _____ can help in the afternoon.
   a. Alex   b. David   c. Gio
4. They are going to move Liz's boxes _____ .
   a. into the living room   b. upstairs   c. downstairs
5. There is _____ on the floor.
   a. paint   b. a stain   c. water damage
6. The light _____ .
   a. isn't turning on   b. was flickering   c. is too bright
7. The _____ in the bathroom needs to be fixed.
   a. sink   b. toilet   c. shower
8. Yoko broke _____ .
   a. her nail   b. the picture   c. the lightbulb
9. Alex didn't _____ .
   a. use a towel   b. turn off the water   c. try to fix anything

DVD 40
VHS 34:05
−36:03

D Watch the video and match the sentences with the things they refer to. (You will use some things more than once.)

1. The landlord got someone to come in and fix it. ____
2. Yoko says the landlord should have it repaired. ____
3. It needs to be screwed in tighter. ____
4. It keeps dripping. ____
5. It might need to be replaced. ____
6. It's loose. ____
7. Maybe it just needs tightening. ____
8. It needs to be taken down. ____

a. the floor
b. the knob on the faucet
c. the lightbulb
d. the picture
e. the refrigerator
f. the showerhead

DVD 41
VHS 36:30
−36:53

E Listen to this conversation. What do the characters say exactly? Cross out the extra letters and words.

Gio   OK. ~~Have you~~ got that end?
Yoko Just a second. Ow! That hurt!
Gio   Are you OK?
Yoko Yeah, I'm fine. I just broke a nail.
David Do you need help?
Yoko No, I think we can handle it. Thanks
        anyway. OK.
Gio   Are you ready?
Yoko Let's try it again. Uh-huh.
Gio   1, 2, 3, lift.

After you watch

A **What can you remember? Answer the questions.**

1. What repairs have been done in the apartment?
   _____

2. What does Yoko need to do before she moves out?
   _____

3. What should the landlord do?
   _____
   _____

B **Look at the picture. Write six sentences about what needs to be done.**

1. <u>The hole in the wall needs fixing / to be fixed.</u> _____
2. _____
3. _____
4. _____
5. _____
6. _____

C **Write some sentences about things that need to be done in your home. Use your own ideas and the words in the box.**

clean	fix	lamp	repair	tighten	wash
faucet	floor	lightbulb	replace	walls	window(s)

_____

_____

_____

Tell a partner about what needs to be done. Which of the jobs above would you do yourself? Which would you have done?

"The windows are dirty. They need to be washed. I'll probably do that myself."
"The walls in the living room need painting. I'm going to hire someone to do that."

Act 3

Before you watch

A Read the money tips. Underline the words and expressions related to money. Then put them in the chart.

Money tips from our readers

I always <u>have a monthly budget</u>, and I stick to it. I keep track of all my money. And I always make sure to put some money away for a rainy day.
– Keesha, Phoenix, AZ

You should never borrow money from a friend. But if you do, always pay the loan back quickly!
– Ralph, Tampa, FL

If you're having money problems, it may help to give up some things. You don't want to get into debt – it's too hard to get out of it!
– Michael, Los Angeles, CA

Don't charge too much on your credit card. It's much better to pay in cash.
– Cindy, Denver, CO

Things you should do	Things you shouldn't do
have a monthly budget	

B Match the sentences with the responses. Then practice with a partner.

1. It's hard to stick to a budget sometimes. _____
2. What did Lucy ask you? _____
3. I want to go on vacation, but I don't know if I can afford it. _____
4. I used to be more of a spender than a saver, but I'm trying to change my spending habits. _____
5. What did he say when you asked him to pay back the money? _____

a. I had a similar experience. I had to learn how to keep track of my money.
b. I know what you mean. It *is* hard.
c. He was like, "No problem. I'll write you a check right now."
d. That's like when I went to Italy. I didn't have a lot of money, so I stayed in youth hostels.
e. She asked me if I was going to buy a new car soon.

While you watch

DVD [42]
VHS 37:17
−41:38

A Check (✓) true or false. Then try to correct the false sentences.

1. Yoko hates moving.
   ☑ True ☐ False
   _____

2. She's moving into a one-bedroom apartment.
   ☐ True ☐ False
   _____

3. Yoko's parents are helping her.
   ☐ True ☐ False
   _____

4. David thinks it's easy to save money.
   ☐ True ☐ False
   _____

5. Yoko will be living with a new roommate.
   ☐ True ☐ False
   _____

6. David has had trouble paying his bills before.
   ☐ True ☐ False
   _____

7. Gio had to give up a few things.
   ☐ True ☐ False
   _____

8. Yoko spends about eighteen dollars a month on coffee.
   ☐ True ☐ False
   _____

9. The friends are going out for coffee.
   ☐ True ☐ False
   _____

DVD [43]
VHS 37:37
−40:17

B Who does or has done these things? Check (✓) the correct people. For some answers, more than one person will be checked.

Who . . . ?	David	Gio	Yoko
1. needs / needed to buy things for a new apartment			
2. hasn't put enough money away for a rainy day			
3. is more of a spender than a saver			
4. tries to set aside money each month			
5. has / had a monthly budget			
6. got into debt			
7. was spending too much money			

While you watch

DVD 44
VHS 37:17
–41:38

C Listen for these sentences. Match the sentences with the responses.

1. Are you almost ready for your move? __a__
2. What's your new place like? _____
3. I don't know how I'm going to be able to afford everything. _____
4. So are you going to be OK – moneywise, I mean? _____
5. I'm sure you'll be able to pay it back quickly. _____
6. Do you have, um, a monthly budget or anything? _____
7. Oh, no. So, what did you do? _____
8. So, you were saying . . . about giving things up? _____
9. That's like, seventy dollars a month. _____
10. It'll save us some time and money. _____

a. I guess so.
b. I hope so.
c. I think so.
d. Oh, uh, not really.
e. Sounds good.
f. That's like when I moved.
g. Yeah, well, speaking of coffee . . .
h. Well, it's a studio apartment.
i. I had to change my spending habits.
j. Wow! Yeah. Just from making one small change.

DVD 45
VHS 37:17
–39:42

D Who says each sentence and what does it refer to? Circle the correct name and then match the sentence to its topic.

1. "But still, it was stressful!"
   (Gio)/ **David** / **Yoko** says this about _____ .
2. "Oh, that's really generous of them."
   Gio / **David** / **Yoko** says this about _____ .
3. "I wouldn't worry about it too much."
   Gio / **David** / **Yoko** says this about _____ .
4. "It makes me a little nervous."
   Gio / **David** / **Yoko** says this about _____ .
5. "I had one in the past. . . . I just could never stick to it."
   Gio / **David** / **Yoko** says this about _____ .

a. a monthly budget

b. living and paying rent alone

c. moving

d. taking money

e. loaning money

DVD 46
VHS 39:23
–40:17

E Listen to this conversation. What do Yoko, David, and Gio say exactly? Complete the sentences.

David What did Gio say?

Yoko He (1) _____ whether or not I had a monthly budget. And I don't.

David Oh. Yeah, having a budget is (2) _____ . I learned that a few years ago when I had some money problems. To make a long story short, I got into some real (3) _____ and had trouble paying my bills.

Yoko Oh, no. So, what did you do?

David I had to change my spending (4) _____ – learn how to (5) _____ of my money. That kind of thing.

Gio Exactly. I had a (6) _____ experience. When I moved here and went back to school, I realized I was (7) _____ too much money. So, I had to give up a few things.

After you watch

A What can you remember? Answer the questions.

1. Why is Yoko worried about money?

   _____

2. What is Gio's advice to Yoko?

   _____

3. What are some other ways that Yoko can save money?

   _____

B Work with a partner. Choose one of the situations and role-play a conversation.

Situation 1

Student A: You are a student. You don't have a budget, you spend a lot, and you charge a lot to a credit card. You don't think you need to worry about money right now – you can think about it after you graduate. Explain this to your friend – Student B.

Student B: You are a student. You keep track of money, pay your bills, and don't buy things you can't afford. You are worried about your friend – Student A. Give your friend advice about money and tell him / her to be more careful. Start like this: *I'm worried about you. . . .*

Situation 2

Student A: You have a budget and usually stick to it. You need to buy a car for a new job, but you can't quite afford it. A good friend – Student B – has a lot more money than you. You want to ask your friend to loan you the money to buy the car. Explain your plan to pay the money back. Start like this: *I have a favor to ask you. . . .*

Student B: Your friend – Student A – wants to borrow some money. You have enough to loan the money. Ask questions to find out how and when your friend will pay the money back. Then decide whether you will loan the money or not.

C Work in small groups. Write down the best advice anyone has ever given you about money. Then compare your advice. Who has the best advice?

_____

_____

_____

_____

_____

_____

_____

"My grandmother told me to put aside a little money every week. She said . . ."

Episode 4 Follow Your Dream

Act 1

Before you watch

A Complete the definitions with the words in the box.

bad press	making a name
celebrity	✓ media
downhill	producer
dropped out of sight	the headlines
gig	up-and-coming

1. The _media_ is a word used to describe TV, radio, newspapers, and the Internet.
2. A person who is famous is often called a _____ .
3. A person who provides money for a movie or a recording is a _____ .
4. An informal word for a performance or a concert is a _____ .
5. A person who is becoming well known is an _____ star. People often say this person is _____ for him or herself.
6. A person who is in the news a lot at the moment is in _____ .
7. Someone who is not in the news any more has _____.
8. A person who has unflattering things written about him is getting _____ . After that, his career might go _____ .

B Match the sentences and the tag questions.

1. It's a beautiful day, _g_   a. do we?
2. It's not five o'clock already, ____   b. doesn't he?
3. Tom Richards lives in Hollywood, ____   c. doesn't she?
4. He got married last year, ____   d. didn't he?
5. You haven't seen his new movie yet, ____   e. didn't she?
6. Liz sings jazz, ____   f. is it?
7. She moved to Los Angeles, ____   g. isn't it?
8. We should get to the concert early, ____   h. have you?
9. We don't have enough time, ____   i. couldn't you?
10. You could call a taxi, ____   j. shouldn't we?

While you watch

DVD 47
VHS 41:43
−46:41

A Circle the correct answers. For some items, both answers are correct.

1. Yoko hasn't talked to Liz because **Liz / Yoko** has been busy.
2. David is reading a celebrity magazine for **fun / research**.
3. Luke Richards is in **the headlines / a new movie**.
4. Before she moved to L.A., Liz was working as a **Web designer / singer**.
5. Liz has already **performed in some big clubs / recorded her first album**.
6. David and Gio say that Liz was discovered by a **producer / club owner**.
7. Liz has met some **up-and-coming stars / interesting musicians**.
8. Liz is looking for **a new manager / new songs**.

DVD 48
VHS 41:43
−46:15

B Who says these things? Check (✓) the correct names.

	Alex	*David*	*Liz*	*Yoko*
1. *It's a little strange being here without Liz, though.*				
2. *Um, it's about how the media has changed the nature of fame.*				
3. *Whoa! Everybody come here a minute.*				
4. *Now Liz is living her dream.*				
5. *It sounds like her career is already taking off.*				
6. *Well, we're all at the park today, and we miss you so much!*				
7. *It says that you're an up-and-coming star . . .*				
8. *But I'm a little concerned about next month.*				
9. *But, you know, nobody really knows who I am yet.*				

DVD 49
VHS 42:19
−44:04

C Watch the video. Then check (✓) Liz or Luke to answer the questions.

	Liz	*Luke*
1. *Who is someone to watch?*		
2. *Who is doing a lot of volunteer work?*		
3. *Who was in the right place at the right time?*		
4. *Who has dropped out of sight?*		
5. *Who got a lot of bad press?*		
6. *Who is making a name for him / herself?*		

While you watch

D Listen for these sentences. Circle the ones you hear.

1. a. It's great to just hang out in the park, isn't it?
   b. It's been great to just hang out in the park, hasn't it?
2. a. You must really miss her.
   b. You really miss her, don't you?
3. a. He completely dropped out of sight for a while.
   b. He kind of dropped out of sight for a while, didn't he?
4. a. You guys have seen it, haven't you?
   b. You guys haven't seen it, have you?

DVD 51
VHS 45:08
–46:41

5. a. The one in *Wow Magazine*?
   b. That one in *Wow Magazine*, right?
6. a. So, everything's going OK?
   b. So, everything's going OK, isn't it?
7. a. You should talk to your manager, don't you think?
   b. You should talk to your manager, shouldn't you?
8. a. I mean, are you going to be recording your album soon?
   b. I mean, you're going to be recording your album soon, aren't you?
9. a. I mean, can't you sing some of your old songs?
   b. I mean, you could sing some of your old songs, couldn't you?

DVD 52
VHS 41:43
–45:34

E Listen for these sentences. Match the sentences with the ones that follow them.

1. How's she doing in Los Angeles? _____
2. What's happening in the celebrity world? _____
3. So, what's he up to these days? _____
4. What is it? _____
5. It's amazing, isn't it? _____
6. It's not too early to call, is it? _____
7. Sounds pretty great, doesn't it? _____
8. He's supposed to get you gigs and get your name out there, right? _____

a. Oh, no!
b. There's something in here about Liz!
c. Yeah, it does!
d. I don't know!
e. Uh, not much.
f. I mean, it's pretty lucky that she was singing in the club that night.
g. Well, this article says he's doing a lot of volunteer work now.
h. Yeah. And he is.

After you watch

A What can you remember? Answer the questions.

1. What has Liz been doing in Los Angeles?

   _____

2. What is she worried about?

   _____

3. What do you think will happen?

   _____

B Add tag questions to complete the conversation. Then practice with a partner.

A Look at this. . . . Tom Richards has a new movie out.

B Tom Richards? He won an Oscar this year, (1) _didn't he_____ ?

A Yeah, he did. And now he's made another movie.

B That's not the one about the horse ranch, (2) _____ ?

A Yeah, they filmed it in Australia.

B Oh, it looks a bit like California, (3) _____ ?

A Yeah, I guess so. . . . You've been to Australia, (4) _____ ?

B Yeah. I went a couple of years ago.

A You went to Sydney, (5) _____ ?

B Uh-huh. . . .

A That's where Tom Richards lives, (6) _____ ? You could have gotten his autograph while you were there!

B Oh, come on!

C Complete the sentences with your own information. Then compare with a partner.

1. If I had / hadn't met _____ ,

   I would / wouldn't have _____ .

2. If I had / hadn't gone _____ ,

   I would / wouldn't have _____ .

3. If I had / hadn't been _____ ,

   I would / wouldn't have _____ .

Episode 4 Follow Your Dream

Act 2

Before you watch

A Match the words in the box with the definitions.

an analyst	contacts	a degree	a loan	a salary
an award	✓ a corporation	humanitarian	a résumé	worthwhile

1. a large company: _a corporation_
2. a document that summarizes your education and
   work experience: _____
3. a title given by a university: _____
4. a person who examines facts and gives an opinion: _____
5. a prize for an achievement: _____
6. money that is borrowed and must be paid back: _____
7. regular pay you receive for a job: _____
8. people you know who can help you find a job: _____
9. concerned with improving the lives of other people: _____
10. meaningful, useful, or valuable: _____

B Complete the conversation with expressions from the box.
Use correct capitalization.

✓ the best thing to do	what I mean	what the job involves	what we should do
the good thing about that	what she's been doing	what we really need	what you're saying

A What do you think of hiring Penny for the job?

B Hmm. I'm not sure that that's (1) _the best thing to do_ .
   She's pretty green.

A What do you mean, exactly?

B Well, (2) _____ is that she's a
   recent college grad and has only been at her current job for a year.
   (3) _____ is someone with more experience.

A I understand (4) _____ , but I
   think Penny is someone who can grow with the company. Plus, if you look at
   (5) _____ , it's very similar to
   (6) _____ at her current job.

B Well, I think (7) _____ is to hire someone
   else to manage the project, but hire Penny for the assistant position.

A That makes sense. (8) _____ is that we
   can give her a chance.

While you watch

DVD 53
VHS 46:46
−50:56

A Circle the correct answers.

1. Gio has finished his _____ .
   a. exams   b. job search

2. A company in _____ is interested in Gio.
   a. town   b. Chicago

3. _____ is more important to Gio.
   a. Making a lot of money   b. Doing something worthwhile

4. Alex has heard of _____ .
   a. the company in Chicago   b. East Cliff Bank

5. Henry Willets works as _____ .
   a. an analyst   b. a stockbroker

6. After Gio sent his résumé, he followed up with _____ .
   a. a phone call   b. an e-mail

7. Alex's friend got a job by _____ a lot.
   a. interviewing   b. calling

8. Yoko knows Henry Willets because _____ .
   a. he's a customer   b. she uses East Cliff Bank

9. Yoko says the next time she sees Henry she'll _____ .
   a. talk to him   b. call Gio

DVD 54
VHS 46:46
−50:56

B Who does these things? Check (✓) the correct names.

Who . . . ?	Alex	David	Gio	Kim
1. hasn't said congratulations yet				
2. hasn't made any decisions yet				
3. asks Gio where he'd like to work				
4. asks if the bank won an award				
5. thinks Gio should go for it				
6. thinks Gio should talk to everyone he knows				
7. thinks companies don't like you to call them				
8. asks Yoko if she knows Henry Willets				
9. says it never hurts to ask friends for help				

While you watch

DVD 55
VHS 47:11
–48:47

C Watch the video and check (✓) the correct answers.

Which company . . . ?	Company in Chicago	East Cliff Bank
1. did Gio send a follow-up e-mail to		
2. does humanitarian work		
3. is a big corporation		
4. is interested in Gio		
5. gives small loans to poor people		
6. offers a great starting salary		

DVD 56
VHS 46:46
–49:16

D Who says each sentence and what does it refer to? Circle the correct name. Then match the sentence to its topic.

1. "Why don't we start anyway?"
   Alex / **Gio** says this about _____ .

2. "It feels pretty good to finally be done."
   Alex / **Gio** says this about _____ .

3. "I have a couple more to go."
   Alex / **Gio** says this about _____ .

4. "Isn't it here in town?"
   Alex / **Gio** says this about _____ .

5. "I think you should go for it."
   Alex / **Gio** says this about _____ .

6. "But I am not very comfortable asking my friends for help like that."
   Alex / **Gio** says this about _____ .

a. East Cliff Bank

b. getting a job at East Cliff Bank

c. eating lunch

d. finishing exams

e. getting personal contacts

f. going on interviews

DVD 57
VHS 47:43
–49:45

E Listen for these sentences. Match the two parts to complete them.

1. I guess what I'm saying is _____
2. What his department does is _____
3. I think what you should do is _____
4. Something a friend of mine did was _____
5. I need to do more if I want the chance to _____

a. talk to everyone you know.
b. give small loans to poor people all over the world.
c. work for Henry Willets.
d. interesting.
e. I want to use my business degree to do something worthwhile.

After you watch

A What can you remember? Complete Gio's notes about the two jobs.

Company in Chicago

One advantage: _____

One disadvantage: _____

East Cliff Bank

One advantage: _____

One disadvantage: _____

B What would you do if you wanted to work at a particular company? Rank each of these suggestions from 1 (very useful) to 5 (not useful at all).

1. do research about the company and the work that it does _____
2. call the company regularly to ask if there are any positions available _____
3. send an e-mail to ask if there are any positions open _____
4. send a résumé by e-mail _____
5. write a letter or e-mail saying why you would like to work for the company _____
6. contact the president or the CEO of the company directly _____
7. develop a personal contact at the company _____
8. volunteer to work at the company for free (an internship) _____

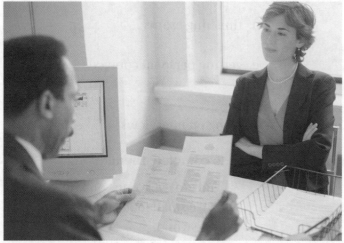

C Give a friend advice about getting an interview at a particular company. Complete the sentences using the ideas in Exercise B and your own ideas.

1. The first thing you should do is _____
2. The advantage of that is _____
3. Another important thing is _____
4. The main reason to do that is _____
5. Something a friend of mine did was _____
6. What I would do is _____

D Work in small groups. Compare your answers to Exercises B and C above. Do you agree with the advice?

Act 3

Before you watch

A Match the words in the box with the definitions.

ban	gallery	mayor	quality of life
✓ construction	livable	pollution	restless

1. the process of putting up new buildings and structures: <u>construction</u>
2. unable to relax or stay in one place: _____
3. something that makes air or water dirty: _____
4. a room or building where art is shown: _____
5. the leader of a town or city: _____
6. the level of comfort and enjoyment of a group of people: _____
7. to forbid something officially: _____
8. enjoyable to live in: _____

B Use the words in parentheses to complete each sentence with the passive form of the present continuous or present perfect. (Pay attention to time words in the sentences.)

1. *A* Four new apartment buildings <u>have been built</u> (build) in the past year.
   B Oh, that's good. People need more places to live.
2. *A* Hundreds of trees _____ (plant) around the city recently.
   B Oh, I've noticed. They look beautiful!
3. *A* The old City Hall _____ (tear down).
   B Oh, that's too bad. It was a historic building.
4. *A* Private cars _____ (ban) from the city center permanently.
   B Really? Has it helped with traffic?
5. *A* Several new office buildings _____ (put up) in the next year.
   B Oh, do we really need more office buildings?
6. *A* A new house _____ (build) next door to mine right now.
   B That's nice.

While you watch

A What topics are mentioned? Circle the correct topic in each pair.

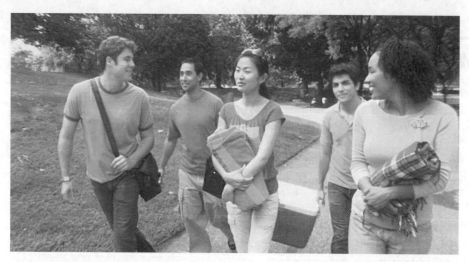

DVD 58
VHS 51:01
–55:49

1. a. the mayor's plan
   b. the mayor's election
2. a. building parks
   b. planting trees
3. a. new construction
   b. new city jobs
4. a. crime
   b. pollution
5. a. writing a novel
   b. shooting a movie

6. a. finding money
   b. winning the lottery
7. a. opening a restaurant
   b. opening a gym
8. a. learning a language
   b. teaching art
9. a. running a company
   b. running a gallery
10. a. good friends
    b. a good job

B Listen for these sentences. Match the two parts to complete them.

DVD 59
VHS 51:36
–52:47

1. What I heard is that ____
2. Well, it'll be great to have more trees –
   especially because ____
3. Even though all this new construction is good
   for the city, ____
4. The reason I ask is, you know, ____
5. Well, what I was going to say was ____
6. So instead of driving everywhere, ____

a. a lot of older buildings have been
   destroyed.
b. the noise and pollution are getting
   pretty bad.
c. they want to plant fifty thousand new
   trees over the next five years.
d. so many new buildings are being put
   up.
e. people would use public transportation
   or walk.
f. that part of the plan is to ban private
   cars from the city center on weekends.

While you watch

DVD 60
VHS 51:01
−55:49

C Listen for these sentences. Match the underlined words and the things they refer to.

1. I wish there were more places like <u>this</u> in the city. _____
2. <u>It</u>'s supposed to help make the city more livable. _____
3. <u>It</u>'s a shame because some of those buildings were historic. _____
4. See, I think <u>that</u>'s great. _____
5. <u>That</u> sounds good, David, but, um, how are you going to pay your bills? _____
6. But <u>it</u> may be hard. _____
7. <u>That</u>'d be cool. _____
8. <u>It</u> was fun. _____

a. the mayor's plan
b. banning cars
c. the park
d. writing a novel
e. running a gallery
f. destroying buildings
g. going to the park
h. owning a restaurant

D Watch the video and complete the conversations with the correct form of the verbs in the box. (You may need to add auxiliaries *be* or *have.*)

be	go back	run	work
change	graduate	teach	write

DVD 61
VHS 52:47
−53:34

Kim   Do you know what you're going to do in ten years? Or even five years?

Gio   I don't even know what I'm doing tomorrow.

Kim   No, seriously. What do you guys think you'll be doing? Where do you think you'll (1) _____ ?

David   In five years? To be honest, I have no idea. I suppose I'll (2) _____ jobs again. You know how I get restless. Or maybe I'll have quit (3) _____ and I'll (4) _____ a novel.

DVD 62
VHS 54:16
−54:54

Alex   And hopefully, in five years, I'll (5) _____ with a degree in fine arts. So, maybe I'll (6) _____ art to kids, or . . .

Kim   Or you might (7) _____ a gallery or something.

Alex   Yeah. That'd be cool!

Gio   You want to go back to school, Alex? That's funny. I will have finally graduated, and you'll (8) _____ .

After you watch

A What can you remember? What is one thing each person says about what he or she will be doing in five or ten years?

1. David   _Maybe he'll have changed jobs again._
2. Gio   _____
3. Yoko   _____
4. Alex   _____

B Think about a city or neighborhood you know well. Write three or four sentences about what is being done and what has been done to improve the city or neighborhood. Use the categories in the box to help you. Then compare answers.

apartment buildings	cars and traffic	public services
bike trails	houses	roads and transportation
buildings (old and new)	public areas	trees and parks

_____

_____

_____

_____

"About fifty new trees have been planted in my neighborhood, and a new park has been created. A bike trail is being built to cross the city."

C Work in small groups. Discuss these questions.

1. What is something new you will be starting in the near future?
2. What is a project you'll be working on in the next six months?
3. What is something you will have finished in the next year?
4. What do you think you'll be doing in five years?
5. What is a dream you would like to have accomplished in ten or twenty years?

Illustration credits

Carlos Castellanos: 4, 24, 32
Chuck Gonzales: 25, 29
Marilena Perilli: 9, 12, 16, 37

Photography credits

1 ©Walter Hodges/Getty Images
5 (*top to bottom*) ©Alamy; ©Jupiter Images
8 (*left to right*) ©Inmagine; ©Ryan McVay/Getty Images
13 ©John Elk/Getty Images
17 ©Inmagine
19 (*bottom row, all*) ©Inmagine
21 (*both*) ©Jupiter Images
36 ©Jupiter Images
44 ©Jupiter Images
45 (*both*) ©Inmagine

Irregular verbs

Base form	Simple past	Past participle
be	was/were	been
beat	beat	beaten
become	became	become
begin	began	begun
bite	bit	bitten
bleed	bled	bled
blow	blew	blown
break	broke	broken
bring	brought	brought
build	built	built
burn	burned/burnt	burned/burnt
buy	bought	bought
catch	caught	caught
choose	chose	chosen
come	came	come
cost	cost	cost
cut	cut	cut
dig	dug	dug
do	did	done
draw	drew	drawn
dream	dreamed/dreamt	dreamed/dreamt
drink	drank	drunk
drive	drove	driven
eat	ate	eaten
fall	fell	fallen
feed	fed	fed
feel	felt	felt
find	found	found
fight	fought	fought
fly	flew	flown
forget	forgot	forgotten
forgive	forgave	forgiven
freeze	froze	frozen
get	got	gotten
give	gave	given
go	went	gone
grow	grew	grown
hang	hung	hung
have	had	had
hear	heard	heard
hide	hid	hidden
hit	hit	hit
hold	held	held
hurt	hurt	hurt
keep	kept	kept
know	knew	known
lead	led	led
leave	left	left
lend	lent	lent
let	let	let
lie	lay	lain

Base form	Simple past	Past participle
light	lit	lit
lose	lost	lost
make	made	made
mean	meant	meant
meet	met	met
pay	paid	paid
prove	proved	proven/proved
put	put	put
quit	quit	quit
read	read	read
ride	rode	ridden
ring	rang	rung
rise	rose	risen
run	ran	run
say	said	said
see	saw	seen
sell	sold	sold
send	sent	sent
set	set	set
sew	sewed	sewn/sewed
shake	shook	shaken
shine	shone	shone
shoot	shot	shot
show	showed	shown/showed
shut	shut	shut
sing	sang	sung
sink	sank	sunk
sit	sat	sat
sleep	slept	slept
speak	spoke	spoken
speed	sped	sped
spend	spent	spent
spill	spilled/spilt	spilled/spilt
spring	sprang	sprung
stand	stood	stood
steal	stole	stolen
stick	stuck	stuck
strike	struck	struck
swim	swam	swum
take	took	taken
teach	taught	taught
tear	tore	torn
tell	told	told
think	thought	thought
throw	threw	thrown
understand	understood	understood
wake	woke	woken
wear	wore	worn
win	won	won
wind	wound	wound
write	wrote	written